INCREDIBLE
UNIVERSE
VOLUME 1: THE SOLAR SYSTEM

Alex McColgan, Stewart McPherson and Robert Irving

Publication Details

Incredible Universe - Volume 1: The Solar System
ISBN 978-1-913631-06-2

All rights reserved. First printed December, 2021

Published by The Don Hanson Charitable Foundation
www.donhansoncharitablefoundation.org

While reasonable efforts have been made to ensure that the
contents of this educational resource are factually correct,
the Don Hanson Charitable Foundation does not accept
responsibility for the accuracy or completeness of the
contents, and shall not be liable for any loss or damage that
may be occasioned directly or indirectly through the use of, or
reliance on, the contents of this educational resource.

All links to websites were valid during November, 2021.

As content on the websites used in this resource book might
be updated or moved, hyperlinks may cease to function.

In the case of space programmes for various countries, the
current dates of planned missions may change and new
discoveries may revise or adjust findings, figures and theories.

The authors would like to thank Abbie Mitchell and Jennifer
Chalmers for kindly reviewing this work. Also thanks to Carl
Davies for designing artwork in this book.

Image on cover and title page by NASA/Seán Doran
https://www.flickr.com/photos/seandoran

CONTENTS

FOREWORD

We often get caught up in the day to day of life and start to feel closed in by the many chores and problems we face, be it in school, at work, or in our personal lives. But when we get a chance to look up, we see the breathtaking number of stars sparkling in our sky, the dim, distant galaxies, and the impenetrable darkness and vastness of space, it puts the mundane into perspective.

It's not that work and school aren't important – they are – but looking up from time to time helps us understand that there is so much more beyond our immediate surroundings. We are part of something much bigger, much grander.

We live in a fascinating world, located in a fascinating Solar System, in a galaxy, teaming with stars and planets just waiting to be explored. And beyond that, a Universe containing a wealth of mysteries.

Humanity knows more than it ever has done about the wonders out there, yet there's still so much to be learned. For instance, what is the nature of dark energy and dark matter? Is there life beyond Earth, or are we alone? And if so, what made us special? The next frontier is space exploration, the next age is the space age, and among us are the pioneers that will pave the way to an even more exciting future.

I hope in this book we can capture the magic of space for you as it has captured us. When I was young, I was amazed about the incredible images we have of the planets in our Solar System, which is why a lot of this book is dedicated to these images specifically. Take your time to imagine the immense size and scale of these objects. Imagine what it would be like to stand or float in one and be exposed to the crazy conditions on other worlds, based on the facts you learn in this book.

And afterwards, I hope you won't forget to keep looking up.

Alex McColgan, founder of Astrum YouTube Channel.

PS: A big thank you to all Astrum subscribers out there in the Universe, who brighten the world with their shared love and enthusiasm for the beauty of space, science, and continuous learning!

ONLINE RESOURCES

Explore the Solar System online - visit the Astrum YouTube channel to access hundreds of specially-crafted films that complement this book.

Scan the following QR code

or search 'Astrum' on www.youtube.com

SPECIAL THANKS

Sincere thanks to the Don Hanson Charitable Foundation and the Phillips Foundation for enabling the donation of one copy of this book to each of 8,000 schools in the UK and 4,000 schools across Australia.

For information, please visit www.hansonbox.org and www.rootsandshoots.org.au

www.donhansoncharitablefoundation.org

the
**Phillips
Foundation**

Education changes lives

www.thephillipsfoundation.org.au

THE WONDER OF IT ALL

Since prehistory, humankind has gazed with wonder at the night sky.

Beyond admiring the beauty of those small, twinkling lights, there has always been a desire by the thinkers through the ages to study and to catalogue, and by doing so, to increase our knowledge and understanding of the jewels of the infinite starscape above.

Out of the darkness of the Second World War came the technology for humanity's most stupendous achievement to date: two astronauts from the *Apollo 11* spacecraft landing on the Moon in July 1969, followed by their safe return to Earth. Through this undertaking, we gained a new perspective, not only of ourselves, but of the fragile blue orb upon which, all of our lives depend.

The five decades since the last lunar landing have seen astronomers and space agencies around the globe explore many of the most awe-inspiring questions of science, among them: our place in the Universe, the scale of space and the age of all that we can see.

Mankind has alway had an innate curiosity which drives our need to investigate, question and enquire. Our eyes will forever be looking upwards and outwards, and our rapid advances in technologies and scientific processes in recent decades have accelerated the quest to find out more about our own planet and the Solar System in which it resides.

We are on the precipice of an exciting new wave of exploration and discovery, with return missions to the Moon planned and the real prospect of humans landing on Mars dawning on the horizon.

The authors hope this book will enthuse tomorrow's astronomers and space scientists by inspiring awe at the wonder of it all: the seemingly infinite scale, complexity and majesty of our incredible Universe.

The study of space offers an almost limitless field for discovery, and one which the reader can be part.

Gaze upwards, admire and question.

THE OBSERVABLE UNIVERSE

The Observable Universe is an immense spherical region of space which contains all matter that can be detected from Earth or via space-based telescopes and exploratory probes.

The Observable Universe is believed to be 93 billion light-years in diameter (for definition of light year, see page 10). The term 'observable' relates to the detectable electromagnetic radiation from the objects (such as galaxies and stars), which has had time to reach Earth since the beginning of the cosmological expansion. As light travels at 299,792,458 metres per second, the time that elapses for light to travel across part of the interstellar distances may be measured in millions or even billions of years.

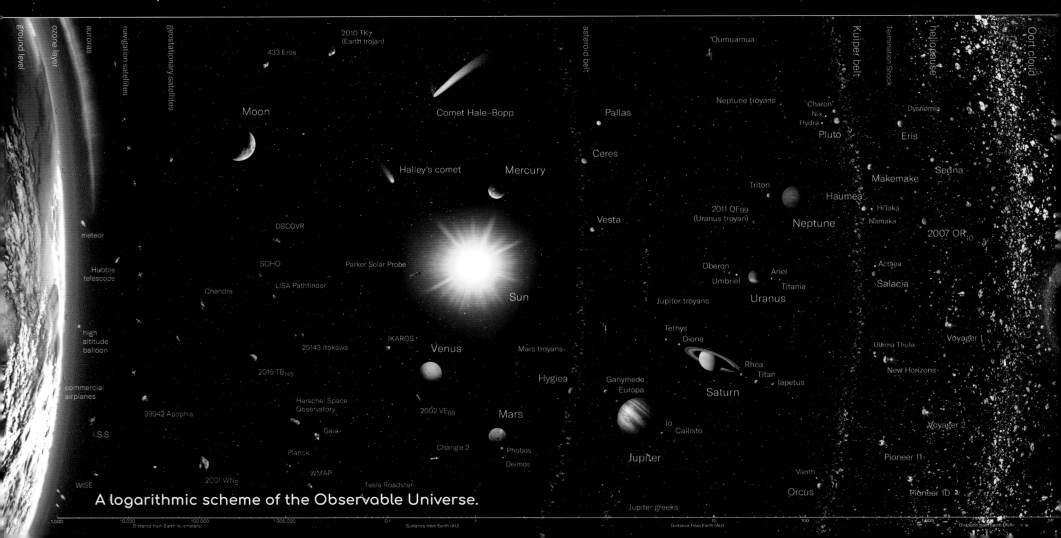

A logarithmic scheme of the Observable Universe.

The most accepted theory of how the Universe began is called the Big Bang. This theory arose when it was found that other galaxies were moving away from our own at great speed and in all directions, as if they had been propelled by an explosive force.

Before the Big Bang, all matter was extremely compact, less than a million billion billionth the size of a single atom. Then, in an unimaginably small fraction of a second, all that matter and energy expanded outward more or less evenly (similar to a big balloon expanding). As time passed and matter cooled, more diverse kinds of particles began to form, and they eventually condensed into the galaxies, stars and planets of the Observable Universe. It is thought the Big Bang happened 13.7 billion years ago.

The nature of space is unknown beyond the limits of the Observable Universe but is thought to be boundless in three-dimensional extents.

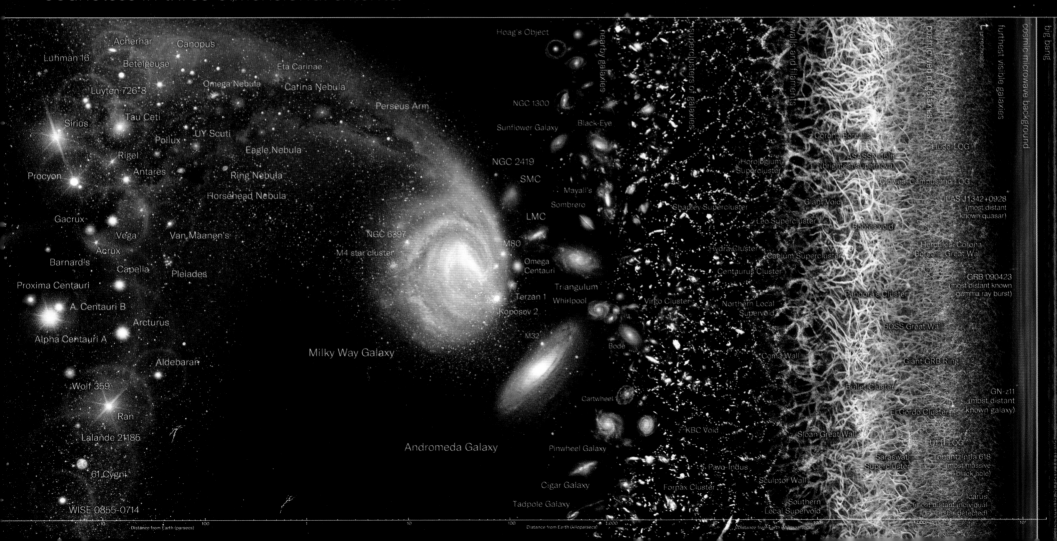

UNIMAGINABLE SCALE

Our Solar System is vast.

Our Galaxy is enormous.

The scale of the Observable Universe is nearly incomprehensible.

Solar System Scale Activity

To consider the size of our Solar System, try undertaking the following activity in a park, your school's grounds or local football field (though you may run out of room after positioning just a few planets!).

Position the following objects in a straight line (in this activity, 1 metre = 6 million km):

1. Inflate a balloon to 20 cm diameter and place this on the ground. This represents the Sun.
2. Walk 9 m from the Sun and place a pinhead on the ground. This represents Mercury.
3. Walk 18 m from the Sun and place a peppercorn on the ground. This represents Venus.
4. Walk 25 m from the Sun and place a peppercorn on the ground. This represents Earth.
5. Walk 38 m from the Sun and place a pinhead on the ground. This represents Mars.
6. Walk 130 m from the Sun and place a chestnut on the ground. This represents Jupiter.
7. Walk 239 m from the Sun and place a hazelnut on the ground. This represents Saturn.
8. Walk 480 m from the Sun and place a peanut on the ground. This represents Uranus.
9. Walk 749 m from the Sun and place a peanut on the ground. This represents Neptune.
10. Walk 1000 m from the Sun and place a grain of 2 mm sand. This represents Pluto.

Now read the following nine pages. Pause and reflect after each page. At the end of these pages, consider the awesome scale of the Universe, the vast expanses of emptiness and the rarity of matter.

Astronomers use 'astronomical units' (AU) and 'light-years' (LY) as measures of the distances in space.

1 AU = 149,597,870,700 m (roughly 150 million km or approximately the distance from Earth to the Sun).
1 LY = is the distance that light travels in a vacuum in one year (365.25 days), which is 9.46 trillion km.

The Earth and the Moon

The Earth has a diameter of 12,742 km. The Moon has a diameter of 3,476 km and is 384,402 km distant from the Earth. **Note:** the diagrams on the following nine pages are not to scale.

The Inner Solar System

The Inner Solar System (comprising Mercury, Venus, Earth, Mars and the Asteroid Belt) lies within half a billion km (3.2 astronomical units) from the Sun. Compared to the rest of the Solar System, the components of the Inner Solar System all lie relatively close to one another.

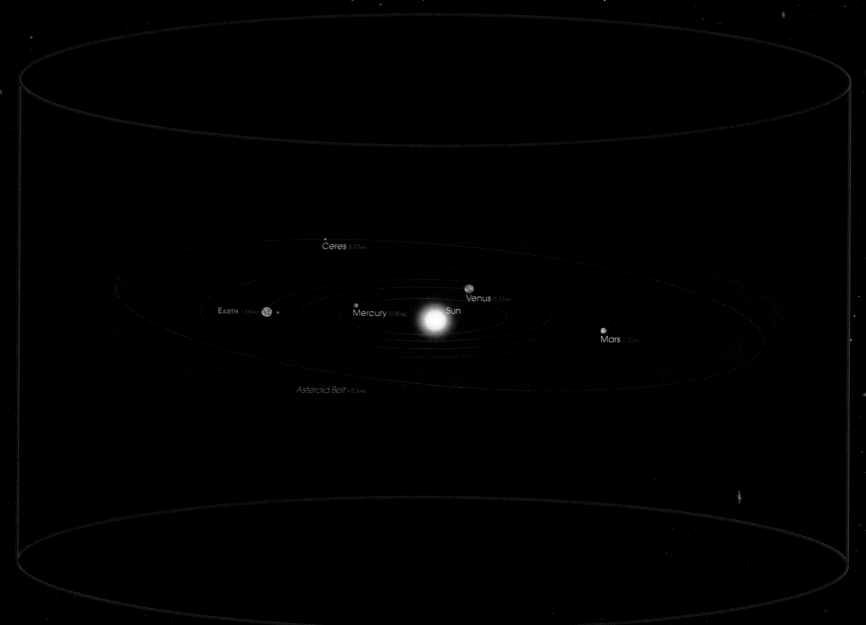

The Outer Solar System

The planets and dwarf planets of the Solar System lie within 14.4 billion km (96.4 astronomical units) from the Sun. The Oort Cloud marks the outer limits of the Solar System, at a distance of up to approximately 15 trillion km (100,000 astronomical units) from the Sun.

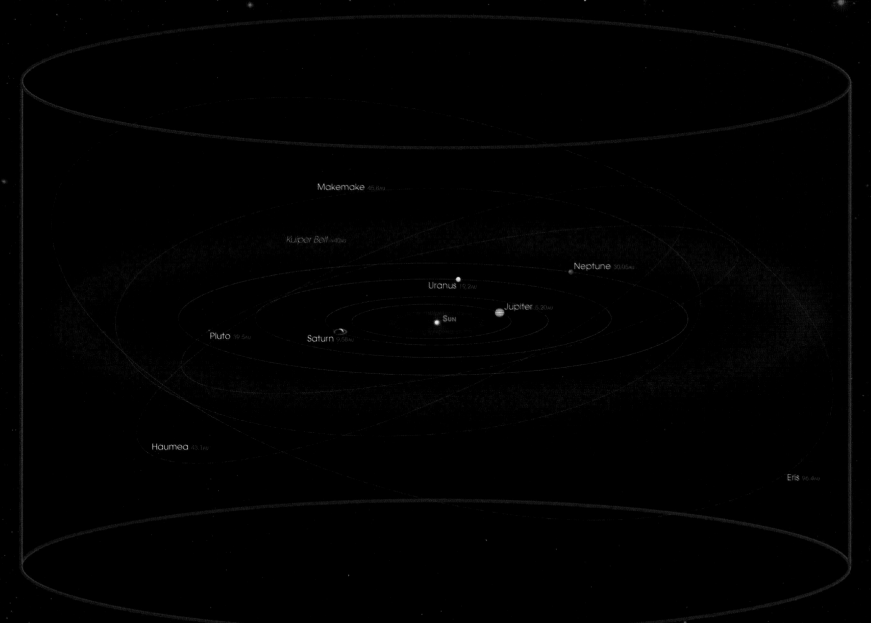

The Closest Stars

Alpha Centauri is a gravitationally bound system of the closest stars and exoplanets to our Solar System. Proxima Centauri is a small, low-mass star located 4.24 light-years from our Sun. Alpha Centauri A and Alpha Centauri B are Sun-like stars, both approximately 4.36 light-years from our Sun.

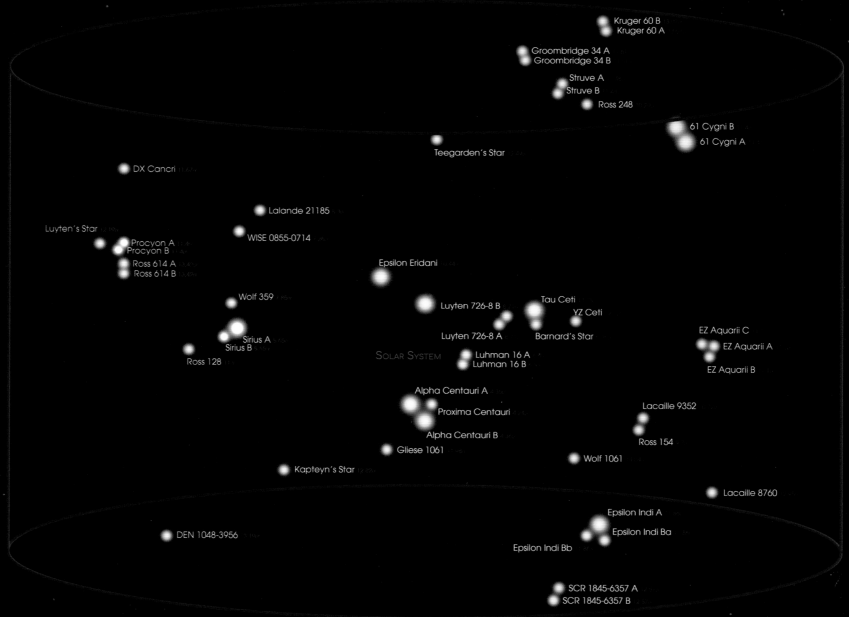

The Milky Way Galaxy

The Milky Way is the galaxy that includes our Solar System. The name describes its appearance from Earth: a hazy band of light seen in the night sky. The Milky Way is a barred spiral galaxy comprising 100 - 400 billion stars with an estimated diameter of 100,000–200,000 light-years.

The Local Group

The Local Group is the galaxy group that includes the Milky Way. It has a total diameter of approximately 10 million light-years. The exact number of galaxies in the Local Group is unknown, however, at least 80 members have been identified, most of which are dwarf galaxies.

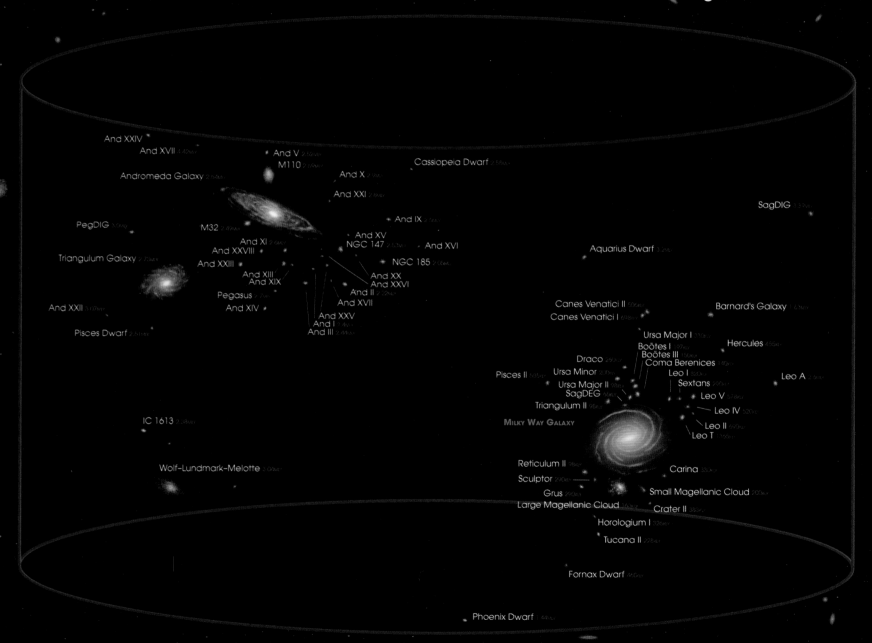

The Laniakea Supercluster

The Laniakea Supercluster is the supercluster of galaxies that is home to the Local Group and approximately 100,000 other nearby galaxies. It spans several hundred million light years and has the mass of 100 quadrillion (10^{17}) Suns.

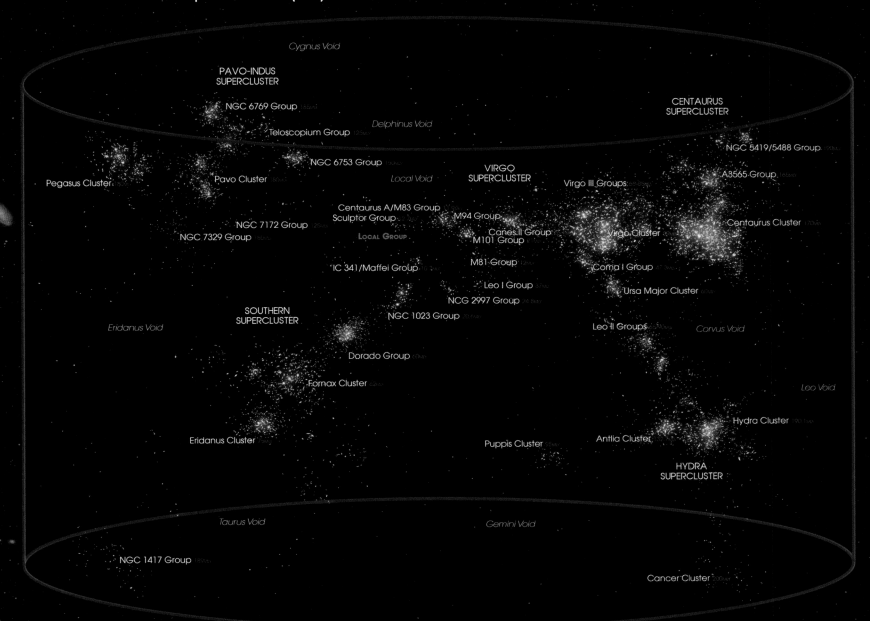

The Local Supercluster

The Local Supercluster (the Virgo Supercluster) contains at least 100 galaxy groups and clusters across an area of over 1,000 million light-years. Just in our Local Supercluster, there are more stars than grains of sand on Earth, and recent findings suggests each star has an average of 10 planets.

The Observable Universe

The Observable Universe is estimated to 93 billion light-years in diameter. About 10 million superclusters are known in the Observable Universe. Recent estimates suggest the Observable Universe may contain more than 2 trillion galaxies. The number of stars and planets is unimaginable.

CROWDED UNIVERSE?

As the previous ten pages demonstrate, the Observable Universe is of immense scale. There are thousands of times more stars in the Observable Universe than grains of sand on every beach on Earth, and all current findings suggest a far greater number of planets. This level of magnitude is beyond human comprehension.

Yet despite the immense number of stars and planets, the distances in space are equally vast. If the average star were shrunk to the size of a grain of sand, the average distance to the next star (4 light-years or about 40 trillion kilometres) would be over 9 kilometres.

It would take our fastest space craft 80,000 years to travel the average interstellar distance. The distance between galaxies is over half a million times greater still. The word 'space' starts to seem very appropriate when you understand the scale of emptiness between stars within our Universe.

When faced with such immense distances and enormous time scales, it may seem as though the dream of human exploration of the Universe will forever be out of reach.

The Age of the Universe

Astronomers can calculate the age of the Universe by several methods of direct observations. One method is to use the rate by which stars cool. By establishing the temperature of the coolest white dwarfs and calculating the rate of cooling, we can establish their age and thereby establish a minimum age of the Universe (as the Universe itself must be at least as old as the oldest objects within it).

Another method is to use measurements of the cosmic background radiation which provide the cooling time of the Universe since the Big Bang.

A third method is to use measurements of the expansion rate of the Universe and thus calculate its approximate age by extrapolating backwards in time. All of these methods can be used to calculate the Universe's age.

The Crab Nebula is a supernova remnant and pulsar wind nebula in the constellation of Taurus.

These (and other techniques) give similar results. As such, astronomers are confident that the Universe is **13.787 billion years old** (with a degree of accuracy of +/- 20 million years). The fact that multiple different dating techniques corroborate one another indicates that these calculations are correct.

Although astronomers can detect the Observable Universe to be approximately 93 billion light-years in diameter, some argue there is evidence to suggest that the outer limits of the Universe may be hundreds of times larger still, or at least 7 trillion light years across.

Whatever its true size, we know the Observable Universe is continually expanding in three dimensions, and according to some, the rate of expansion is ever increasing.

In comparison to the rest of the Universe, our Solar System is relatively young. The Sun formed about 4.6 billion years ago in a giant, spinning cloud of gas and dust called the solar nebula. As the nebula collapsed under its own gravity, it spun faster and flattened into a disk.

Most of the nebula's material was pulled toward the centre to form our Sun, which accounts for 99.8% of our Solar System's mass. Much of the remaining material formed the planets and other objects that now orbit the Sun. (The rest of the leftover gas and dust was blown away by the young Sun's early solar wind.)

The immensity of space and time of the Observable Universe allows us, literally, to see the past among the stars. Here is how:

Some of the most distant galaxies that we can see are more than 10 billion light years away. This means the light was emitted by the stars within those galaxies over 5 billion years before our Sun even formed. In such cases, some of the stars we see are long gone, and by the time the light reflected from Earth travels to those distant galaxies, our Solar System will be long gone.

Indeed, much of our view of the Universe is really looking into the past of galaxies and stars that existed millions or billions of years ago. In this way, we truly can see the past.

These concepts raise perhaps one of the most interesting questions of all - something known as the Fermi paradox.

The Fermi Paradox

There are countless trillions of stars similar to the Sun across the Observable Universe. Most stars have Solar Systems comprising multiple planets. Of the hundreds of stars so far studied, the average number of planets per Solar System is around ten. If even a tiny proportion of these stars have at least one Earth-like planet in a circumstellar habitable zone, there would be billions of habitable worlds across the Universe.

If only a tiny proportion of these habitable worlds evolved life, there would be millions of planets with alien organisms. This is the argument for a crowded universe.

If the Earth is typical and conscious life evolved on other planets, even with technology comparable to the rockets which we can build today, a civilisation could spread across a galaxy within a few million years if it so chose.

Since many stars similar to the Sun are billions of years older, conscious life could have evolved countless times before it emerged on Earth. If so, we should have already been visited by extraterrestrials or at least their probes. Or at the very least, we should be able to detect signatures of alien civilisations in space (such as radiowaves). But there is no evidence of any of this.

Does the Universe hold other worlds of life?

The Fermi Paradox asks: with the probability seemingly stacked so heavily towards immense numbers of worlds that could harbour life, **where are the aliens?**

There are many fascinating possible answers to the Fermi Paradox:

1. The emergence of life (called abiogenesis) may be vastly rarer than we comprehend, and Earth may be the only planet (or one of extremely few planets) where life emerged. In this scenario, the immense number of habitable planets across the Universe is outweighed by the far greater improbability of abiogenesis. Those habitable planets (in spite of their habitability) are simply sterile.

2. Simple life (such as single cellular organisms, or their equivalent) is common on habitable planets throughout the Universe, but conscious life is rare or unique to Earth. Or perhaps life is usually extinguished on planets before it evolves into conscious organisms.

Consider our own circumstances: our Sun is destined to turn into a huge, glowing red giant star and render Earth uninhabitable in around 500 million years (some astronomers argue as little as from 100 million years, others as much as 1 billion years). If conscious life (humanity) had taken 10% more time to evolve on Earth, then it would not have existed at all because it would have been destroyed before it emerged.

Could it be that this is the fate of most (or perhaps all) other planets where life emerges?

3. Or perhaps conscious organisms emerge and develop advanced technology, but rapidly use up their available resources and die out or regress, or through other factors (such as conflict or even their own technology (for example, artificial intelligence)) wipe themselves out.

To date, no direct evidence of extraterrestrial life has been detected, although this does not mean it does not exist. Only an infinitesimally small proportion of the Universe has been surveyed for life.

There are two interesting points to note here:

The first concerns a fascinating experiment that was undertaken in 1952, by a young researcher, Stanley Miller and his supervisor, Harold Urey.

Miller and Urey aimed to recreate conditions believed to have prevailed on primordial Earth. The experiment used water (H_2O), methane (CH_4), ammonia (NH_3), and hydrogen (H_2). The chemicals were all sealed inside a sterile glass flask connected to a 500 ml flask half-full of water. The water in the smaller flask was heated to induce evaporation, and the water vapour was allowed to enter the larger flask. Continuous electrical sparks were fired between two electrodes, in the larger flask, to simulate lightning.

The Miller–Urey experiment created over 20 amino acids, the building blocks of life. The experiment did not create life, nor prove life can be created naturally, but it did show that compounds essential for life as we know it can form naturally, relatively easily and rapidly. It is likely that such circumstances occur on planets beyond Earth.

Does our Solar System support simple life?

The second point concerns the fact that the earlie... undisputed evidence of life on Earth dates from ... least 3.5 billion years ago (although some biologis... cite evidence of life arising as early as 4.41 billion year... ago). In both cases, the fact that abiogenesis occurre... so (relatively) rapidly after Earth's formation 4.54 billio... years ago indicates (but does not prove) life can emerg... easily and quickly when the right conditions occur.

Earth lies within the Solar System's 'habitable zon... (also known as the 'Goldilocks zone'). This zone is th... range of orbits around a star within which a plane... can support liquid water (being neither too hot nor to... cold).

On the basis of what we know of life on Earth, the presence of liquid water is a requirement for lif... We know liquid water occurred on Mars and may even remain on that planet below the surface of th... regolith.

We also know many of the moons that orbit the planets of the Solar System harbour liquid (water) sea... below icy crusts. Could any of these harbour simplistic extraterrestrial life?

The study of life beyond Earth is known as astrobiology. Imagine the ramifications of such a discover... Or even the detection of a signal from another planet. How would our belief systems and religion... change? How would we view ourselves within the Universe?

Equally, imagine the impact of discovering no other life in our Solar System, our Galaxy or the Universe... What would it mean to be completely alone in the vast emptiness of space? Or, if we are to find tha... Earth is the only place where life exists, would it limit our desire to explore deeper into space?

Throughout the following chapters, we will explore the main places in the Solar System whic... astrobiologists speculate might hold the greatest changes of harbouring life: Mars, Jupiter's moo... Europa, Saturn's moons Titan and Enceladus, and Neptune's moon Triton. Additionally, astrobiologist... are searching for fossils of ancient life on Mars.

OUR SOLAR SYSTEM

Our Solar System consists of our star, the Sun, and everything bound to it by gravity. Not only does this include the planets (Mercury, Venus, Earth, Mars, Jupiter, Saturn, Uranus, and Neptune) but also dwarf planets such as Pluto, dozens of moons, and millions of asteroids, comets, and dust.

The word 'solar' comes from the Latin word *solis* meaning the Sun. Up until the Middle Ages, it was generally believed that the Earth was at the centre of the universe and that the planets and the Sun revolved around the Earth.

In 1543, the Polish astronomer and mathematician, Nicolaus Copernicus, proposed that the Sun was actually at the centre and that the planets (including the Earth) revolved around it. This theory had been proposed in the 3rd century BCE by Aristarchus of Samos, but had not been taken up. The acceptance of this 'heliocentric' view was when our true understanding of the Solar System began.

For centuries, we thought our Solar System was the only one where planets orbited a star, but we now know there are countless Solar Systems across the Galaxy. Thousands of 'exo-planets' (planets orbiting other stars) have been detected, and many astronomers believe the majority of stars have Solar Systems similar to the Sun. This would mean countless billions of planets within the Milky Way Galaxy alone!

The Sun formed about 4.6 billion years ago when matter within a 'stellar nursery' (consisting mostly of hydrogen and some helium) underwent a 'gravitational collapse', causing a rotation to start which gradually got faster. Most of the collapsing mass collected in the centre, becoming denser and hotter, eventually forming the Sun.

The remaining mass, consisting mostly of gas and dust, formed a 'protoplanetary disk', influenced by the growing gravitational force exerted by the Sun. Over time, the dust grains began to clump together forming clusters and these in turn clumped together to form even larger bodies. Collisions of these bodies then led to some becoming larger and others breaking apart forming fragments. Thus were born the inner four 'terrestrial' planets of Mercury, Venus, Earth and Mars, which have cores consisting

Further out from the Sun, molecules such as water, ammonia, methane and carbon dioxide could remain in a solid state (when they are referred to as 'ices'). These ices coalesced and formed the cores of the outer planets, which then grew massive enough to capture hydrogen and helium, the most abundant elements. Thus the four 'gas giants' of Jupiter, Saturn, Uranus and Neptune came into being.

Interestingly, for a short time after the outer planets formed, it is thought that they may have been warmed through impacts, friction and radioactive decay. Even Pluto may have once been a liquid ocean world, but all have had time to cool over millions of years.

It is now thought that both Uranus and Neptune were formed when they were closer to the Sun, and that they have since moved away to their present orbits.

The Sun constitutes about 99.86% of the mass of the whole Solar System. Of the remaining 0.14%, almost 99% constitutes the masses of these four outer planets, giving an indication of their huge size, particularly that of Jupiter.

Our Solar System (not to scale).

Our Solar System is much more complex than just a series of planets.

Several planets have moons (defined as 'celestial bodies which orbit a planet or dwarf planet'). Moons vary greatly in size and composition. There are dwarf planets such as Pluto and comets (frozen leftovers from the formation of the Solar System composed of dust, rock and ices).

The Solar System also comprises the Asteroid Belt (a doughnut-shaped ring between the orbits of Mars and Jupiter formed of solid, irregularly-shaped bodies of varying sizes) and the Kuiper Belt (similar to the Asteroid Belt, but which exists at the outer reaches of the Solar System beyond Neptune).

The region surrounding the Sun and the Solar System that is impacted by the Sun's magnetic field and constant flow of particles ('solar wind') is known as the heliosphere. The outer edge of the heliosphere is called the heliopause, which lies around 123 astronomical units (18 billion kilometres) from the Sun.

Beyond the heliopause lies the Oort Cloud, the most distant region of our Solar System. It forms a giant thick-walled bubble made of icy pieces of debris. The outer limit of the Oort Cloud defines the boundary of the Solar System. Beyond the Oort Cloud, the void of interstellar space begins.

The relative sizes of the planets (and the dwarf planet Pluto).

The Sun would be the size of a page of this book at this scale

Mercury
Venus
Earth
Mars

Jupiter

Saturn

Uranus

Neptune   Pluto

Selected moons of the Solar System with Earth for scale.

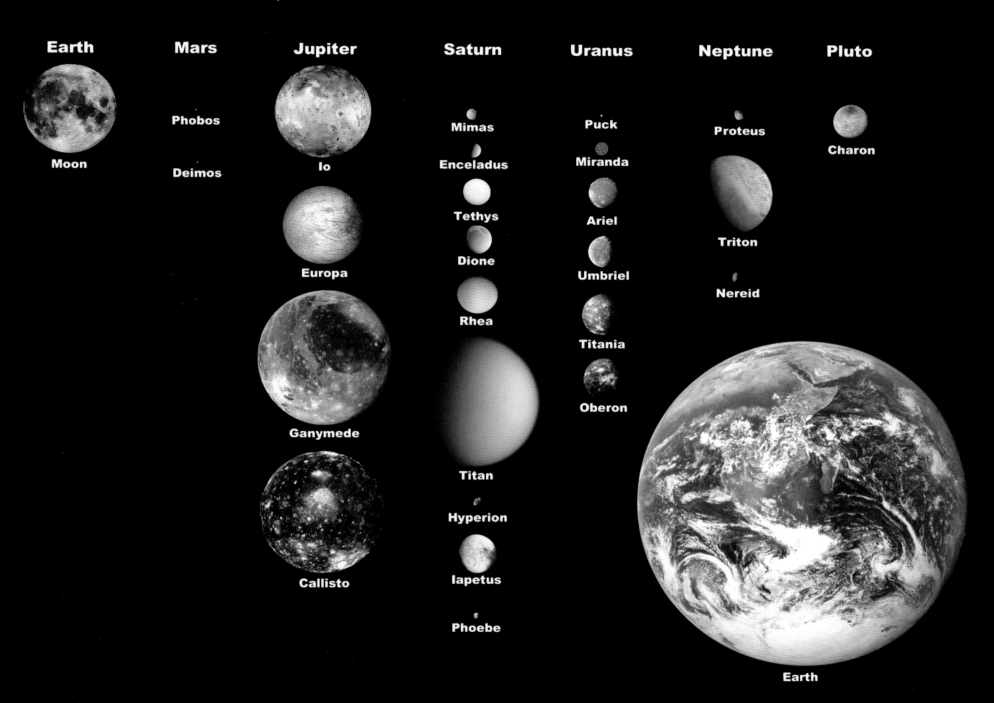

Earth

Moon

Mars

Phobos

Deimos

Jupiter

Io

Europa

Ganymede

Callisto

Saturn

Mimas

Enceladus

Tethys

Dione

Rhea

Titan

Hyperion

Iapetus

Phoebe

Uranus

Puck

Miranda

Ariel

Umbriel

Titania

Oberon

Neptune

Proteus

Triton

Nereid

Pluto

Charon

Earth

Key Facts

	MERCURY	VENUS	EARTH	MARS
First recorded by humanity:	14th century BCE	~1894 BCE	---	2nd millennium BCE
Recorded by:	Babylonian astronomers	1st Babylonian Dynasty	---	Ancient Egyptians
Planet type:	Terrestrial	Terrestrial	Terrestrial	Terrestrial
Distance from the Sun:	57.9 million km	108.2 million km	149.6 million km	227.9 million km
Mass:	0.3301×10^{24} kg	4.8673×10^{24} kg	5.972×10^{24} kg	0.639×10^{24} kg
Equatorial diameter:	4,879.4 km	12,100 km	12,742 km	6,779 km
Surface area:	74.8×10^{5} km^2	460.2×10^{6} km^2	510.1×10^{6} km^2	144.8×10^{6} km^2
Surface temperature range:	-173 ° to +427 °C	up to +480 °C	-88 °C to +58 °C (mean: 16 °C)	-153 °C to +20 °C
Gravity (% compared to Earth):	38% (3.727 m/s^2)	90% (8.87 m/s^2)	9.807 m/s^2	38% (3.721 m/s^2)
Surface Atmospheric Pressure:	Negligible	93 bar	1 bar	0.01 bar
Main atmosphere gases:	No atmosphere present	CO_2 (96%); N_2 (3%)	N_2 (78%); O_2 (21%)	CO_2 (95%); N_2 (3%)
Number of moons:	None	None	1	2
Notable moons:	---	---	The Moon	Phobos; Deimos
Number of rings:	None	None	None	None
Strength of magnetic field:	Moderately strong	Weak	Strong	Very weak
Direction of rotation:	West to East (2° tilt)	East to West (2.6° tilt)	West to East (23° tilt)	West to East (25.2° tilt)
Rotational period (day length):	58 days 15 hrs 30 mins	116 days 18 hrs	24 hrs 0 mins	24 hrs 37 mins
Orbital revolution period (year length):	87.97 Earth days	225 Earth days	365.25 Earth days	687 Earth days

	JUPITER	SATURN	URANUS	NEPTUNE	PLUTO
	8th century BCE	'since ancient times'	1781	1846	1930
	Babylonian astronomers	Rings discovered by Jan Huygens (Holland) in 1659	William Herschel (UK) (though he thought it likely to be a comet)	Johann Galle (Germany) & Urbain Le Verrier (France)	Clyde W. Tombaugh (USA)
	Gas giant	Gas giant	Ice-gas giant	Ice giant	Dwarf planet
	778.6 million km	1.43 billion km	2.87 billion km	4.49 billion km	6 billion km
	$1,898 \times 10^{24}$ kg	568.3×10^{24} kg	86.81×10^{24} kg	102.4×10^{24} kg	1.30900×10^{22} kg
	139,822 km	116,460 km	50,724 km	49,528 km	2,376.6 km
	61.42×10^{9} km^2	42.7×10^{9} km^2	8.083×10^{9} km^2	7.618×10^{9} km^2	16.7×10^{6} km^2
	down to -100 °C	-185 °C to -122 °C	-224.2 °C to -170.2 °C	-201 °C (mean)	-240 °C to -218 °C
	253% (24.79 m/s^2)	106% (10.44 m/s^2)	89% (8.69 m/s^2)	114% (11.15 m/s^2)	6.3% (0.620 m/s^2)
	>1,000 bar	>1,000 bar	>1,000 bar	>1,000 bar	<0.1 bar
	H_2 (90%); He (10%)	H_2 (75%); He (25%)	H_2, He + Methane (CH_4)	H_2 (80%); He (19%); CH_4 (1%)	N_2, CH_4, CO
	at least 75	at least 82	at least 27	at least 14	at least 5
	Io; Europa; Ganymede; Callisto	Titan; Iapetus; Rhea; Dione	Titania and Oberon	Triton; Hippocamp; Proteus	Charon; Hydra; Nix
	Faint rings present	Seven main rings	13 known faint rings	Six narrow rings known	None
	Very strong	Slightly weaker than Earth's	Moderate but offset	Very strong, though offset	Presence of magnetic field not known
	West to East (3° tilt)	West to East (26.7° tilt)	East to West (on its side: 98° tilt)	West to East (28.3° tilt)	East to West (57° tilt)
	9 hrs 56 mins	10 hrs 42 mins	17 hrs 14 mins	16 hrs 6 mins	6.39 Earth days
	4,333 Earth days	10,585 Earth days	30,660 Earth days (84 Earth years)	60,152 Earth days (164.8 Earth years)	90,582 Earth days (248 Earth years)

A Saturn V
rocket takes off.

Left and right
Nazi V-2 rockets.

Apollo 15 Saturn V Stage Separation.

OUR JOURNEYS TO SPACE

The idea of humans venturing into space dates back centuries.

Archytas (428 to 347 B.C.), a Greek astronomer, was said to have constructed and flown a small bird-shaped device that was propelled by a jet of steam or compressed air. The 'bird' may have been suspended by a wire or mounted at the end of a bar that revolved around some sort of pivot. But regardless, this was the first reported device to use rocket propulsion.

For over 2,000 years, Chinese chemists experimented with gunpowder, and by 1232, primitive rockets were attached to arrows and used to repel Mongol invaders in the battle of Kai-keng.

The French science fiction writer Jules Verne (1828 to 1905) wrote *De la Terre á la Lune*. In this story, a giant cannon was used to fire a crewed projectile at the Moon. Although not a rocket, the projectile was called the Columbiad and contained a crew of three. Verne correctly described how the crew would feel 'weightless' on their voyage, and Verne's vivid account fired the public imagination of space flight.

But it was during the darkest hours of the Second World War that rocket technology was truly born. Adolf Hitler's Nazi regime turned rockets from science fiction novelties to sophisticated weapons of destruction. The first true ballistic missile, known as the V-2, was developed in the 1930s and 1940s under the direction of Wernher von Braun.

The V-2 rocket became the first man-made object to travel into space by crossing the Kármán line on 20th June 1944. The Kármán line marks the boundary between Earth's atmosphere and outer space, beginning 100 km above Earth's mean sea level.

Beginning in September 1944, over 3,000 V-2s were launched by the German forces against allied targets, particularly London, causing an estimated 9,000 civilians deaths.

At the end of the Second World War, teams from the allied forces raced to seize the main German manufacturing facilities, procure Germany's missile technology, and capture the V-2's launching sites.

Rocket expert Wernher Von Braun and over 100 key V-2 personnel surrendered to American forces. Many ended up working in American research programmes to develop similar rocket weapons for the US Air Force. Later, their early rocket designs contributed towards the founding of the American space agency, the National Aeronautics and Space Administration (NASA).

The end of the Second World War marked the start of another conflict, this time between the USA and the USSR, though one where subterfuge, espionage and propaganda replaced large military campaigns.

By the late 1950s, the Russians were ahead. In October 1957, they successfully launched *Sputnik*, the world's first man-made satellite into orbit, and in 1961, the Soviet cosmonaut Yuri Gagarin became the first person to orbit the Earth.

But in May 1961, US President John F. Kennedy made the bold claim that the USA would land a man on the Moon by the end of the decade. In an inspiring speech on September 12th, 1962, he proclaimed:

> *'We choose to go to the Moon in this decade and do the other things, not because they are easy, but because they are hard; because that goal will serve to organize and measure the best of our energies and skills, because that challenge is one that we are willing to accept, one we are unwilling to postpone, and one we intend to win.'*
>
> John F. Kennedy

To achieve this goal, NASA launched the *Apollo* programme and developed the colossal *Saturn V* multi-stage rocket. A series of test flights were conducted to prepare for the mission to the Moon.

Sadly, a major setback occurred in 1967, when a cabin fire killed the entire 3-man crew aboard *Apollo 1* during a pre-launch test. This flight was intended to be the first crewed mission of the programme, but the engineers of NASA identified the causes of the fire and enhanced the design of future vehicles.

December 1968 saw the launch of *Apollo 8*, the first manned spacecraft to orbit the Moon. Then on 20th July 1969, *Apollo 11* landed two astronauts (Neil Armstrong and Buzz Aldrin) on the Moon. A third astronaut (Michael Collins) remained on the command module orbiting the Moon.

This incredible feat effectively meant that the USA had won the space race.

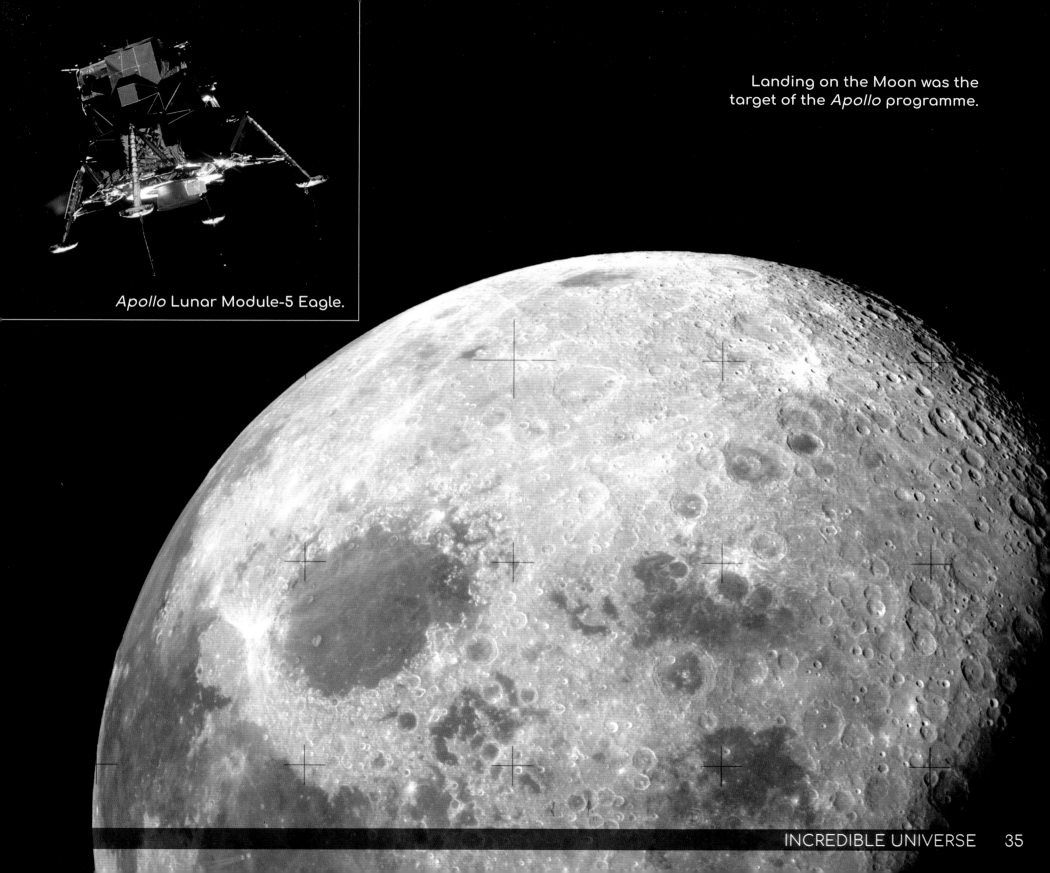

Landing on the Moon was the target of the *Apollo* programme.

Apollo Lunar Module-5 Eagle.

The landing of humans on the surface of the Moon has been the most stupendous achievement in the history of humankind. Just consider the incredible complexity of this accomplishment and its significance; not for warfare or conquest, but the advancement of science and knowledge.

Grainy black and white video beamed back to Earth as *Apollo 11*'s Lunar Module *Eagle* touched down on the Moon's surface on July 20, 1969. The engine shut off, Neil Armstong and Buzz Aldrin celebrated with a brisk handshake and pat on the back, and *Eagle* was depressurised so the hatch could be opened.

Armstrong made his way down the ladder and stepped off the lunar module and onto the surface of the Moon. As he did, he said: '*That's one small step for man, one giant leap for mankind*.'

An estimated 530 million people viewed the lunar landing on televisions around the world (20 percent of the world's population at that time).

Armstrong and Aldrin planted the flag of the USA, collected samples of moon rocks, undertook experiments and took photographs, then returned to Earth safely.

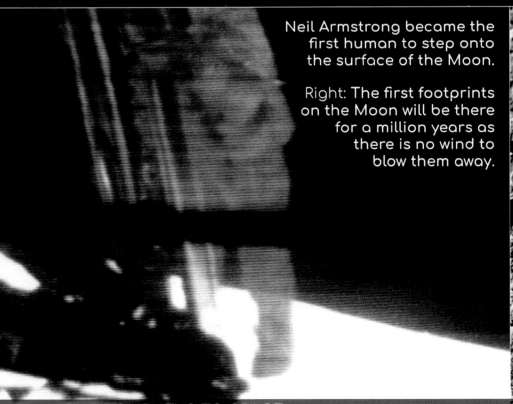

Neil Armstrong became the first human to step onto the surface of the Moon.

Right: The first footprints on the Moon will be there for a million years as there is no wind to blow them away.

Buzz Aldrin removing the passive seismometer from a compartment in the SEQ bay of the Lunar Lander.

A photo called 'Earthrise', taken by *Apollo 8* crewmember Bill Anders on December 24, 1968.

Astronaut Eugene Cernan makes a short checkout of the Lunar Roving Vehicle (LRV) during the early part of the first *Apollo 17* mission, 12 December 1972.

A Lunar sample (Moon rock) on display at NASA's Johnson Space Center.

The first space shuttle launch on April 12, 1981. Astronauts John Young and Robert Crippen spent 54 hours in Earth orbit.

After *Apollo 11*'s successful landing, ten astronauts from five further missions (*Apollo 12, 14, 15, 16* and *17*) have landed on the Moon to date. During many of these missions, the surface of the Moon close to the landing sites has been explored via 'moon buggies', and a total of 382 kg of lunar rocks and surface material has been brought back to Earth, greatly contributing to the understanding of the Moon's composition and geological history.

One of the greatest impacts of the *Apollo* programme resulted unexpectedly from a photograph taken by astronaut William Anders on December 24, 1968, during an orbit of the Moon as part of the *Apollo 8* mission. Anders's photograph, which was subsequently named 'Earthrise' showed our home planet and some of the Moon's surface (see page 37).

Nature photographer Galen Rowell described it as '*the most influential environmental photograph ever taken*', as it showed or little planet as a blue sphere in the vastness of space and inspired people around the world to contemplate the fragility of Earth and all life that it sustains.

Many heralded the perspective that *Earthrise* gave as the beginning of the environmental movement. Fifty years to the day after taking the photo, William Anders observed, '*We set out to explore the Moon and instead discovered the Earth*.'

In December 1972, *Apollo 17* became the last mission of the *Apollo* programme. Further flights to the Moon had been planned, but were cancelled due to budget cuts and changing priorities. Dreams of bases on the Moon and exploring other parts of our Solar System evaporated over the rest of the 20th Century, but have re-emerged with NASA's Artemis programme (see *The Next Chapter*).

From the 1970s onwards, the USA and the USSR (and, after the break-up of the Soviet Union in 1991, the Russians), have been the main protagonists in the exploration of space. These two super-powers have now been joined by China as having the capability of undertaking crewed spaceflight.

Several other national space agencies have sent unmanned craft to other planets, particularly to Mars. These include the European Space Agency (ESA) and those from Japan (JAXA), India and, most recently, the United Arab Emirates.

Many more nations are now capable of launching satellites into a low-Earth orbit, and many others have set up land-based radio telescope observatories, for example Australia's Parkes Observatory.

Space Stations

A space station is a spacecraft capable of supporting a human crew in orbit for an extended period of time, and is therefore a type of space habitat. Space stations are often built to enable astronauts to undertake experiments and research.

The USSR became the first nation to build a space station under the *Salyut* programme which ran from 1971 to 1986. This was followed by a second station named *Mir* in 1986 which lasted until 2001. Various international astronauts visited *Mir*, including British astronaut Helen Sharman in May 1991.

NASA's first space station was called *Skylab*, was only occupied between May 1983 and February 1984.

The *International Space Station* (*ISS*) was the ninth space station to be inhabited by crews. Its first component was launched in 1998, with its first crew arriving in November 2000. Maintaining a low-Earth orbit, averaging 400 km above our planet's surface, the *ISS* celebrated its 21st birthday in 2021 (and has had human occupants for its entire life in orbit).

The *ISS* involved five space agencies: NASA (United States), ROSCOSMOS (Russia), JAXA (Japan), ESA (Europe) and CSA (Canada). The station serves as a laboratory for experiments and investigations in astrobiology, astronomy, meteorology, physics and other subjects in a microgravity environment. Up until August 2021, 244 astronauts had visited the *ISS* from 19 countries including 3 Australians.

Its most critical systems are those involved in life-support and include the atmosphere control system (to maintain a gas mix equivalent to that of air at sea level on Earth). The *ISS* travels at a speed of 28,000 km/hr and completes 15.5 orbits per day. It takes about 10 minutes to pass from one horizon to another.

Earth-orbit Satellites

As of May 2021, there have been 11,139 satellites from more than 40 countries launched into an orbit around Earth. Of these, only 7,389 remain in space (many as non-functional, though highly dangerous, 'junk'), while the rest have been (purposefully) burnt up in the atmosphere. About 63% of operational satellites are in low-Earth orbit (<2,000 km altitude), 6% are in a medium-Earth orbit (>2,000 km and <35,786 km) and 29% are in a geo-stationary orbit (at 36,000 km altitude).

Non-military satellites are used for Earth observation, communications, navigation, weather and as space telescopes (the Hubble Space Telescope can be classified as a satellite). In recent years, several satellite 'constellations' have been launched. These consist of several small satellites working together as a system, typically providing complete Earth coverage. One example is the Global Positioning System (GPS). Originally designed for the sole use of the US military, this system has been in place since 1993 and is now commonplace with receivers in many electronic gadgets. Most recently, private companies such as Starlink and OneWeb have launched hundreds of mini-satellites which will provide complete global internet provision.

In September 2021, the *Landsat-9* satellite was launched from California. This is the latest in a series of Earth-observing satellites stretching back almost 50 years. The images and other data they have obtained provide a continuous record of the changing state of our planet. These include the growth of our cities, the spread of farming, the loss of rainforests and the evolving outline of coasts, deserts and glaciers. The programme has allowed scientists to pull out trends over time and, most importantly, the data are free and classified as open access.

Probes and Rovers

The launch of *Sputnik*, the first man-made satellite, in 1957, opened the possibility of sending scientific equipment to other parts of the Solar System. The USSR's *Venera* programme involved the sending of a series of space probes developed by the Soviet Union between 1961 and 1984 to gather information

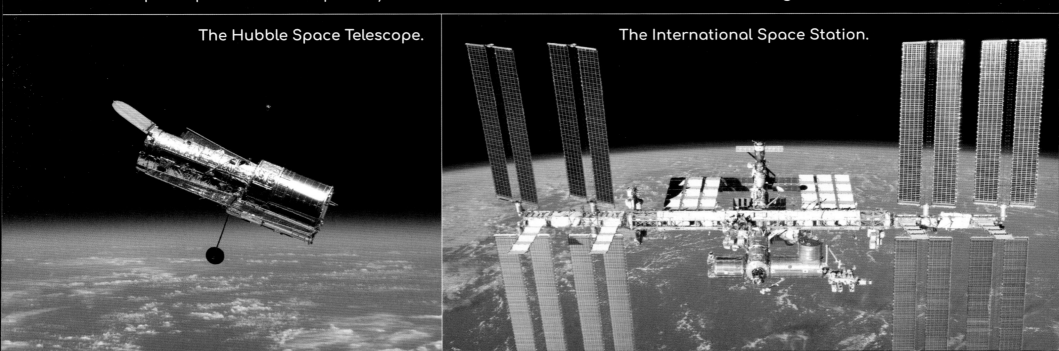

The Hubble Space Telescope.

The International Space Station.

about the planet Venus. Ten probes successfully landed on the surface of the planet, while thirteen probes successfully entered the Venusian atmosphere. These included the first human-made devices to enter the atmosphere of another planet.

During the last fifty years, dozens of spacecraft have been successfully launched and sent to planets and moons throughout the Solar System, including landing rovers (robotic vehicles designed to explore the surfaces of planets or moons remotely).

Two identical probes, *Voyager 1* and *Voyager 2*, were launched in 1977 to study the outer Solar System and have photographed many of the distant planets and their moons. Powered by mini nuclear reactors, as of 2021, the two *Voyagers* are still in operation past the outer boundary of the heliosphere in interstellar space. They both continue to collect and transmit useful data to Earth.

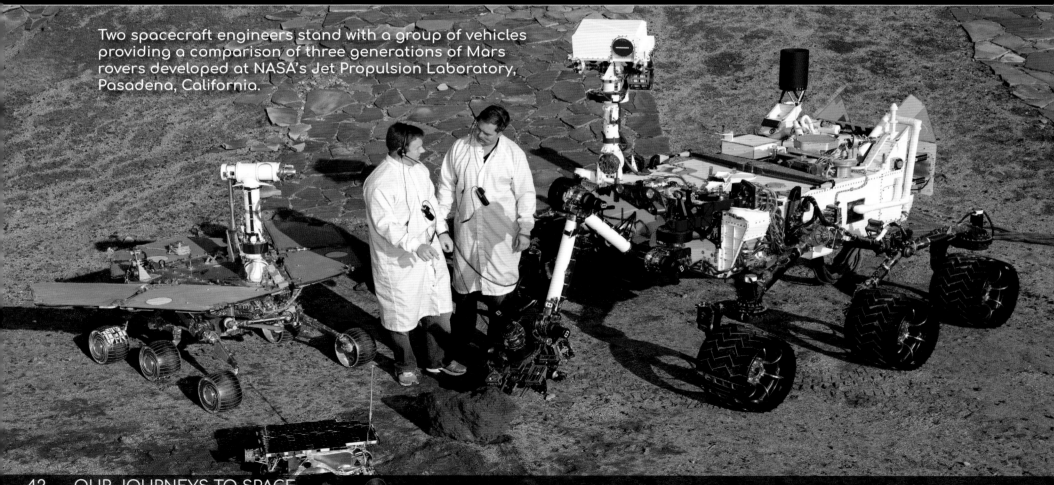

Two spacecraft engineers stand with a group of vehicles providing a comparison of three generations of Mars rovers developed at NASA's Jet Propulsion Laboratory, Pasadena, California.

Since August 20, 1977, *Voyager 2* has been travelling from Earth. As of October 7, 2021, the probe is 128.20 astronomical units (19.178 billion km) distant. It entered interstellar space on November 5, 2018, at a distance of 122 astronomical units but remains functional and in contact with NASA on Earth. *Voyager 2* is not headed toward any particular star, but would take about 80,000 years to travel the distance to Proxima Centauri, the closest star to Earth.

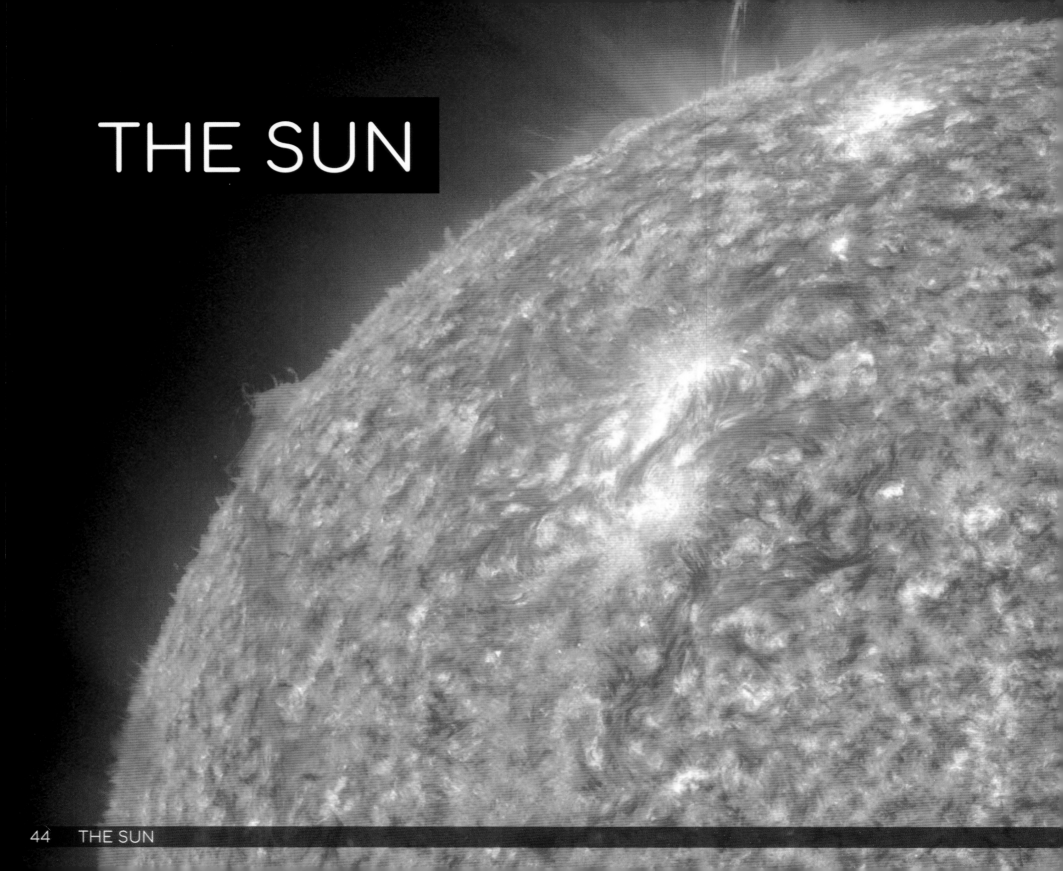

THE SUN

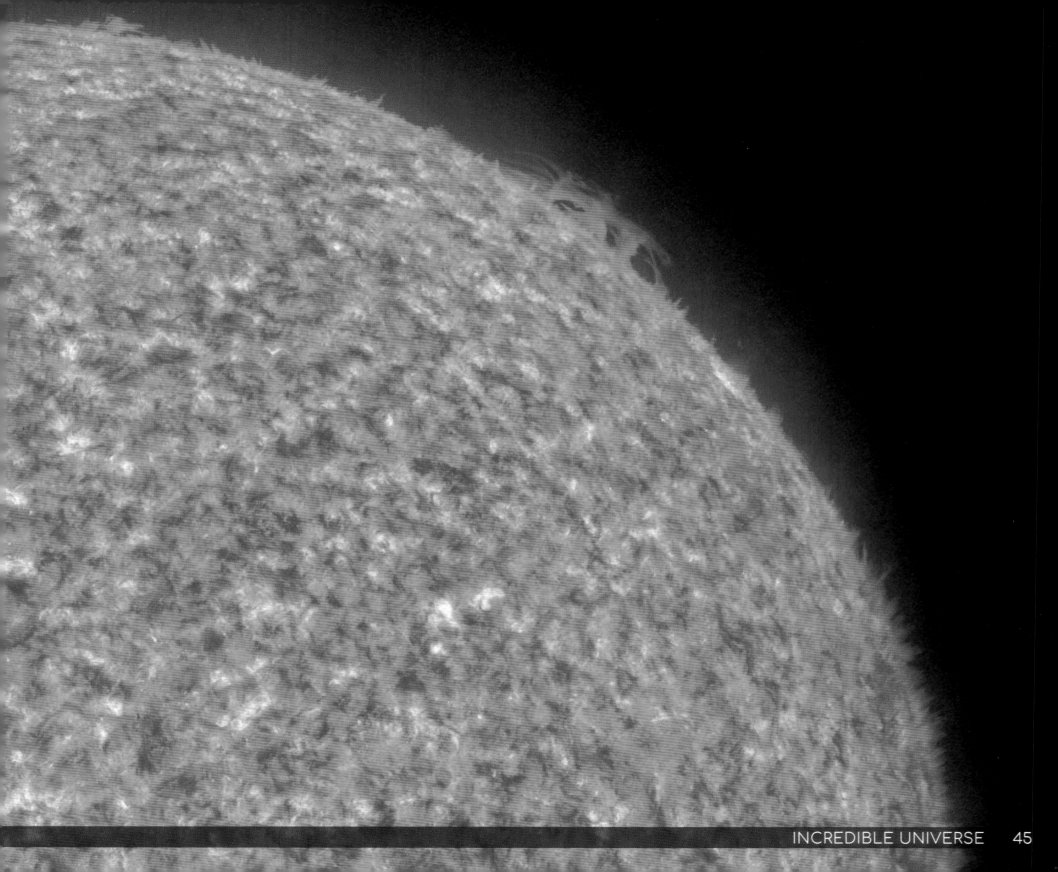

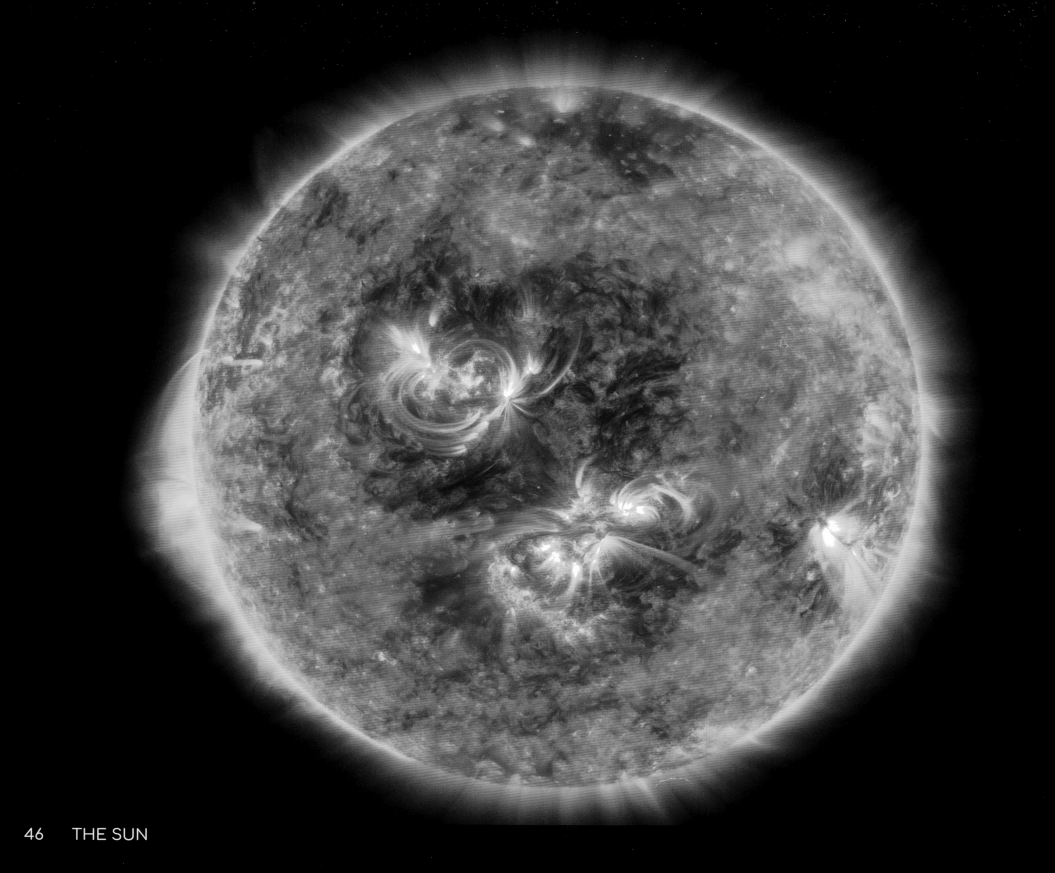

How Big?

Equatorial Diameters

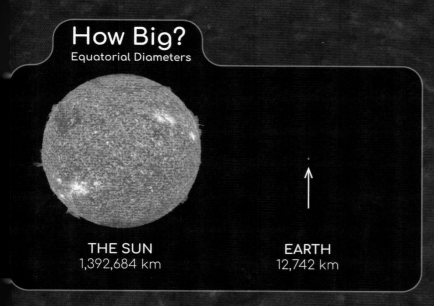

THE SUN
1,392,684 km

EARTH
12,742 km

Key Facts

Constituents:	Hydrogen (75%), Helium (24%), Oxygen (<1%), Other elements (0.1%)
Approximate age:	4.6 billion years
Category of star:	Yellow Dwarf
Diameter:	1,392,684 km
Core Temp.:	15.7 million °C
Surface Temp.:	5,800 °C

The Star at the Centre of our Solar System

The Sun is our local star at the centre of our Sola
System. It appears so much larger and brighte
than all other stars we can see, only because it i
so much closer to Earth.

Technically, the Sun is a 4.5 billion-year-old 'yellov
dwarf star' – a hot glowing ball that consists mostl
of hydrogen and helium. It is, by far, the larges
object in our Solar System and constitutes abou
99.86% of all of the Solar System's matter.

The Sun is about 150 million kilometers from Earth
This distance, known as one 'astronomical unit' (AU
is used as a measure of distance in space. Withou
the Sun's energy, life as we know it could not exis
on Earth.

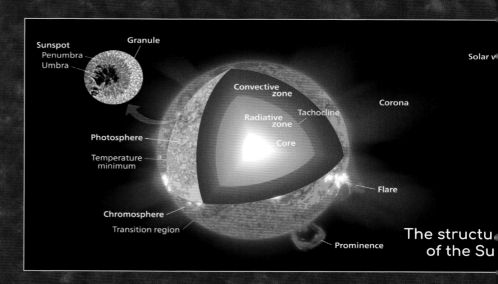

The structu
of the Su

The Sun is estimated to be brighter than about 85% of the stars in the Milky Way Galaxy. The energy from the Sun (which we experience as heat and light, but which also contains other forms of radiation which our bodies are unable to sense) originates from a nuclear fusion process that is occurring in the core of the Sun.

Under conditions of extreme heat and pressure, hydrogen nuclei fuse together to become helium, resulting in a massive release of energy. Some of this energy finds its way to the Sun's surface (though it takes thousands of years to do so) and is released, but most causes more fusion reactions to take place, thus keeping the whole process going. It is estimated that, within the Sun's core, 4.26 million metric tonnes of matter is converted to energy every second.

Because the Sun is a gaseous object, it does not have a clearly defined surface; its visible parts are usually divided into an inner 'photosphere' and an outer 'atmosphere'. Its atmosphere can only really be observed during a solar eclipse, when the Moon lies between the Earth and the Sun, leaving just the outer perimeter of the Sun visible for a few minutes to Earth observers.

The hottest part of the Sun is its core, where temperatures top 15 million °C. The part of the Sun we call its surface – the photosphere – is a relatively cool 5,500 °C. In one of the Sun's biggest mysteries, the Sun's outer atmosphere, the corona, gets hotter the farther it stretches from the surface. The corona reaches up to 2 million °C – much, much hotter than the photosphere.

The Sun has a diameter of about 1.39 million km (864,000 miles) or 109 times that of the Earth. Its mass is about 330,000 times that of the Earth. About 73% of its mass consists of hydrogen, with the rest being mostly helium (~ 25%), with much smaller amounts of oxygen, carbon, neon and iron.

The amount of helium within the Sun's core is gradually increasing. The Sun will continue its present existence for another 5 billion years or so, after which it will morph into its next state, that of being a red giant. As this process unfolds, it will grow considerably in size, subsuming the planets of Mercury and Venus.

The Sun rotates faster at its equator than at its poles. The rotational period is approximately 25.6 Earth days at the equator and 33.5 Earth days at the poles. Viewed from above its north pole, the Sun rotates counter-clockwise around its axis of spin.

The surface of the Sun is highly dynamic.

A solar prominence erupts.

The Sun's atmosphere consists of four distinct parts, one of which, the corona, is responsible for releasing the solar wind. This flow of plasma consists of a stream of charged particles (mostly electrons, protons and alpha particles) which travel at very fast speeds all the way to the edge of the Solar System.

The Sun's corona is very dynamic. From time to time, a giant burst of plasma shoots out from the corona (a phenomenon termed a coronal mass ejection), releasing large quantities of matter and electromagnetic radiation. Should this happen on the side of the Sun facing Earth, it can cause a geomagnetic storm, disrupting the Earth's magnetosphere. This in turn can lead to particularly strong aurorae in the regions around the Earth's magnetic poles, a phenomenon of ethereal dancing colours which we know as the Northern or Southern Lights. The storms can also cause damage to radio transmissions, satellites and to electric power lines.

Solar flares arise as intense eruptions of electromagnetic radiation in the Sun's atmosphere. Flares occur in active regions and are often, but not always, accompanied by coronal mass ejections and solar particle events.

Light from the Sun which reaches the Earth includes infrared, visible and ultraviolet wavelengths. The Earth's atmosphere attenuates (or filters) this light, taking out about 70% of the ultraviolet light. The remaining light is responsible for maintaining life on Earth, primarily through photosynthesis by plants (the process of using energy from sunlight to convert water and carbon dioxide into sugars).

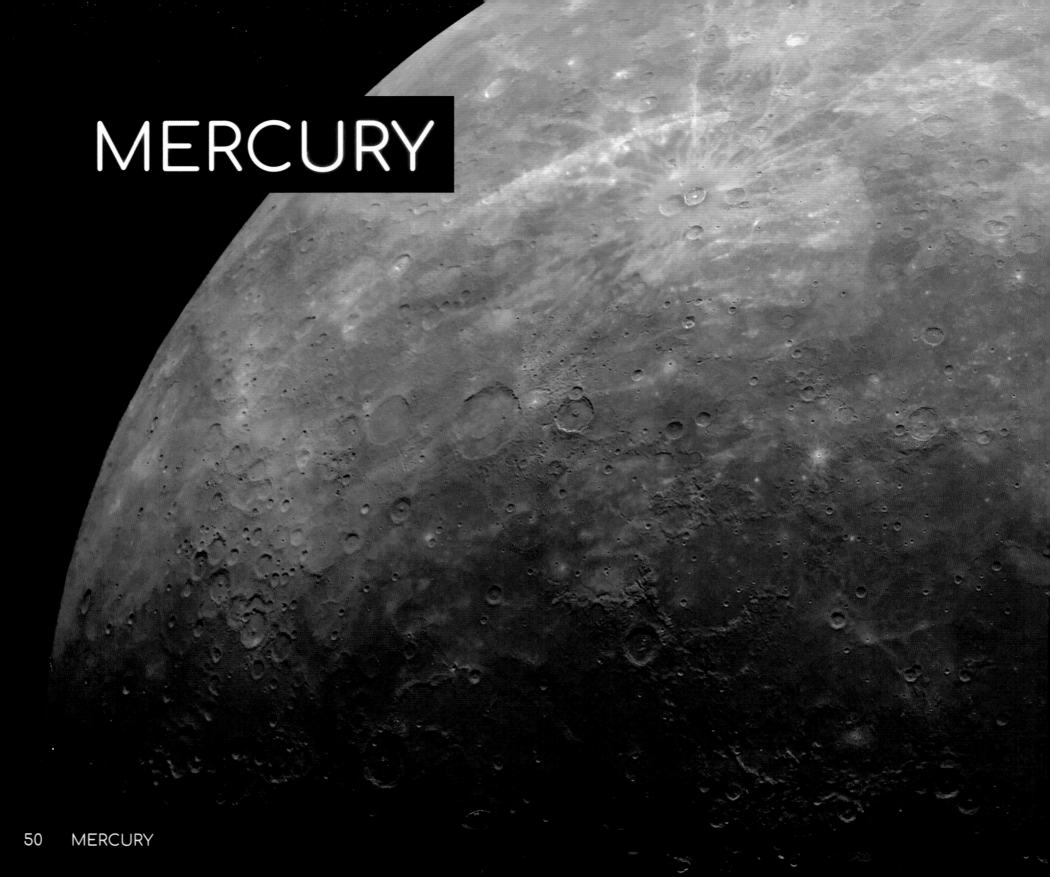

MERCURY

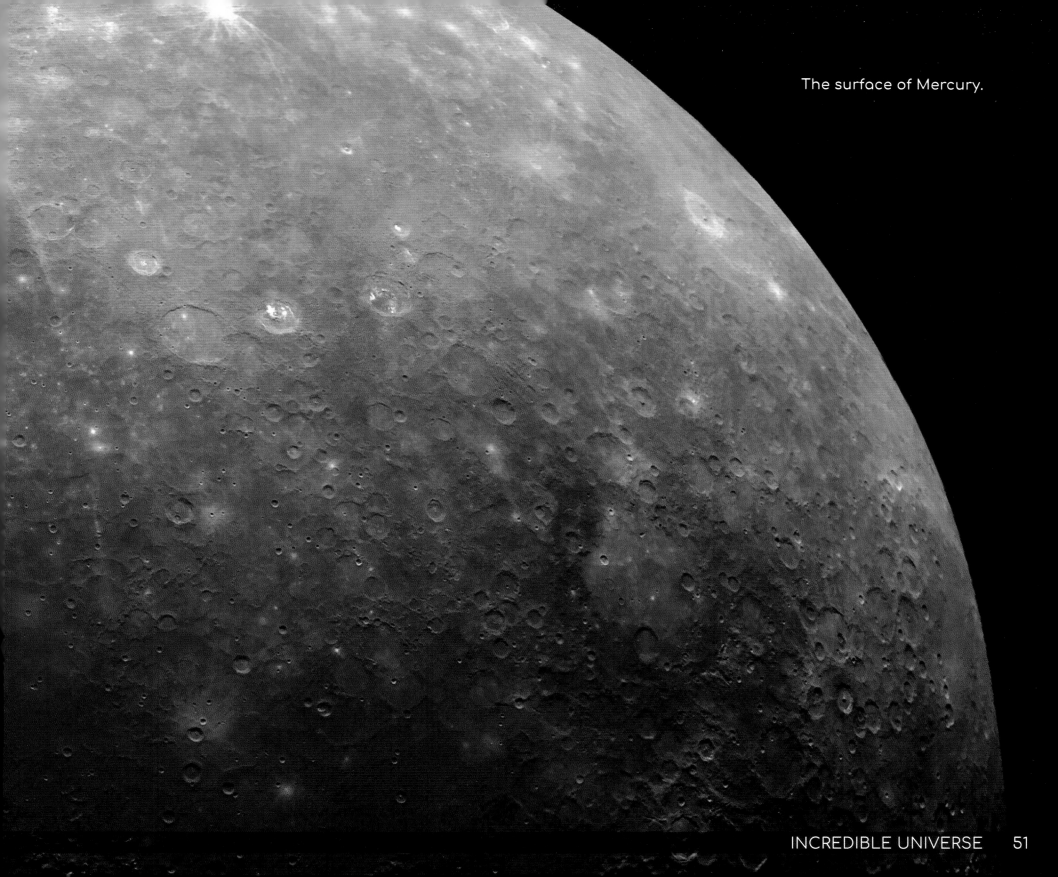

The surface of Mercury.

Mercury is scarred with craters.

How Big?
Equatorial Diameters

MERCURY
4,879 km

EARTH
12,742 km

Atmosphere

No atmosphere but a thin exosphere present.

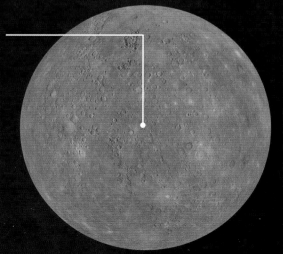

TRACE GASES ────

OXYGEN
(MOLECULAR)

SODIUM

HYDROGEN
(MOLECULAR)

HELIUM
(MOLECULAR)

CALCIUM

POTASSIUM

WATER VAPOUR

Key Facts

First recorded by humanity: **14th century BCE**

First recorded by: **Babylonians**

Planet type: **Terrestrial**

Distance from the Sun: **57.9 million km**

Mass: **0.3301×10^{24} kg**

Equatorial diameter: **4,879.4 km**

Surface area: **74.8×10^{6} km^2**

Surface temperature range: **-173 ° to +427 °C**

Gravity % compared to Earth: **38% (3.727 m/s^2)**

Surface atmospheric pressure: **Negligible**

Main atmosphere gases: **No atmosphere**

Number of moons: **None**

Notable moons: **---**

Number of rings: **None**

Strength of magnetic field: **Moderately strong**

Direction of rotation: **West to East (2° tilt)**

Rotational period (day length): **58 days 15 hrs 30 mins**

Orbital revolution (year length): **87.97 Earth days**

The Closest Planet to the Sun

Mercury is the smallest planet in the Solar System (being slightly larger than Earth's Moon, yet smaller than Jupiter's Ganymede and Saturn's Titan). It is the closest planet to the Sun. However, it is not the hottest, as it has no atmosphere to contain the heat - that accolade goes to Venus. Mercury is named after the Roman god Mercurius, messenger of the gods and capable of swift travel.

True to its name, Mercury also happens to be the fastest planet in our Solar System, travelling through space at 47 km/s (equivalent to 168,000 km/hr!), due to the fact that the closer a planet is to the Sun, the faster it travels. This also means its year is not very long, just 88 Earth days.

Mercury has an elliptical orbit around the Sun. From the planet's surface at its closest approach, the Sun would appear more than three times larger than it does on Earth and its light seven times brighter.

Transit of Mercury. Mercury is visible as a black dot below and to the left of centre. The dark area above the centre of the solar disc is a sunspot.

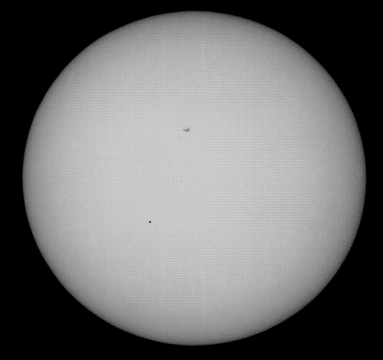

The surface of Mercury.

The planet has a very slow rotation. Its day length lasts for 58 Earth days! This means that at sunrise, the Sun appears to rise briefly, set, and rise again when viewed from some parts of the planet's surface. The same thing happens in reverse at sunset.

Mercury's surface temperatures are both extremely hot and cold. Because the planet is so close to the Sun, day temperatures can reach highs of 430 °C. However, without an atmosphere to retain that heat at night, temperatures can dip as low as -180 °C.

Internal Structure and Exosphere

Mercury has a central metallic core which takes up about 55% of the planet's volume. Surrounding this, the rocky mantle and solid crust are about 400 km thick, about the same as they are on Earth.

Instead of an atmosphere, Mercury possesses a thin exosphere made up of atoms blasted off the surface by the solar wind and striking meteoroids.

Mercury's exosphere is composed mostly of oxygen (O), sodium (Na), hydrogen (H), helium (He), calcium (Ca) and potassium (K). This exosphere is not stable - atoms are continuously being lost and replenished.

Mercury's magnetic field surrounds the whole planet and is about 1.1% the strength of Earth's. It is strong enough to deflect the solar wind around the planet, creating a magnetosphere.

Surface Features

Mercury's greyish-brown surface appears similar to our Moon's, with many impact craters resulting from collisions with meteoroids and comets. There are also extensive smooth areas and some huge cliffs - hundreds of kilometres long and over a kilometre high. There are also 'wrinkle ridges' and compression folds, all formed, it is believed, as the planet's interior cooled and contracted over billions of years.

Mercury's craters range in size from bowl-shaped cavities a few kilometers across to vast, multi-ringed impact basins hundreds of kilometers across. The largest known, 1,550 km in diameter, has been named *Caloris Planitia*. It's one of the largest impact craters in the Solar System.

Mercury is known to have been volcanically active in the past, billions of years ago. The remains of these ancient volcanoes can still be seen within some of the larger craters.

Even though surface temperatures at some points can reach 430 °C, there is thought to be water-ice at the north and south poles inside deep craters, but only in areas where there are permanent shadows.

Missions to Mercury

Reaching Mercury from Earth poses significant technical challenges, because it orbits so much closer to the Sun than Earth. The Sun exerts a gravitational pull on any craft which has to be corrected for. In addition, Mercury is travelling very fast through space, so a large amount of fuel is required to make sure any spacecraft can catch it up.

Picasso crater — the large arc-shaped pit located on the eastern side of its floor is postulated to have formed when sub-surface magma subsided or drained, causing the surface to collapse into the resulting void.

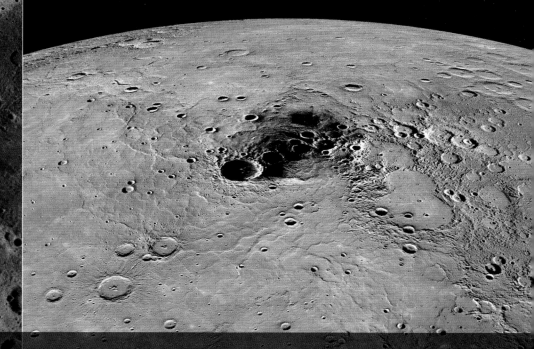

Composite of the north pole of Mercury, where NASA confirmed the discovery of a large volume of water ice within the permanently dark craters that are found there.

To date, there have only been two missions to study Mercury (although a third is currently underway).

The first was NASA's *Mariner 10* (1974-1975) which managed to make three close approaches to the planet. It provided the first close-up images of Mercury's surface. However, the same region of the planet was lit during each pass, resulting in only 45% of the surface being mapped. The craft was also able to measure the planet's magnetic field.

Just eight days after its final approach, *Mariner 10* ran out of fuel and was shut down by its controllers. However, the craft is still thought to be orbiting the Sun, passing close to Mercury every few months.

A second NASA mission to Mercury named *Messenger* departed Earth in August 2004. However, it did not head straight to Mercury. Instead, to increase its velocity, it undertook a series of 'slingshots' around Earth and Venus before it reached Mercury, which it eventually did in January 2008.

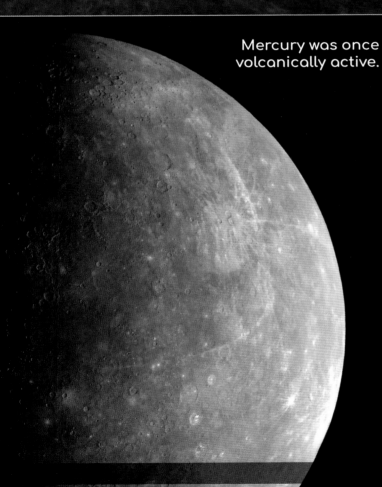
Mercury was once volcanically active.

Three flybys provided imagery of the 'hidden' side of Mercury missed by *Mariner 10*. Much more information was obtained of its geological history, its magnetic field and its exosphere. In 2015, its tasks completed, it was directed to crash into Mercury.

The current mission to Mercury is a joint one by the European Space Agency (ESA) and the Japanese Space Agency (JAXA), using the craft *Bepi-Columbo*. Launched in October 2018, it will settle into orbit around Mercury in December 2025, after numerous flybys to slow down the craft.

Astrobiology

No prospects for supporting life are known from Mercury.

VENUS

The surface of Venus is
obscured by clouds.

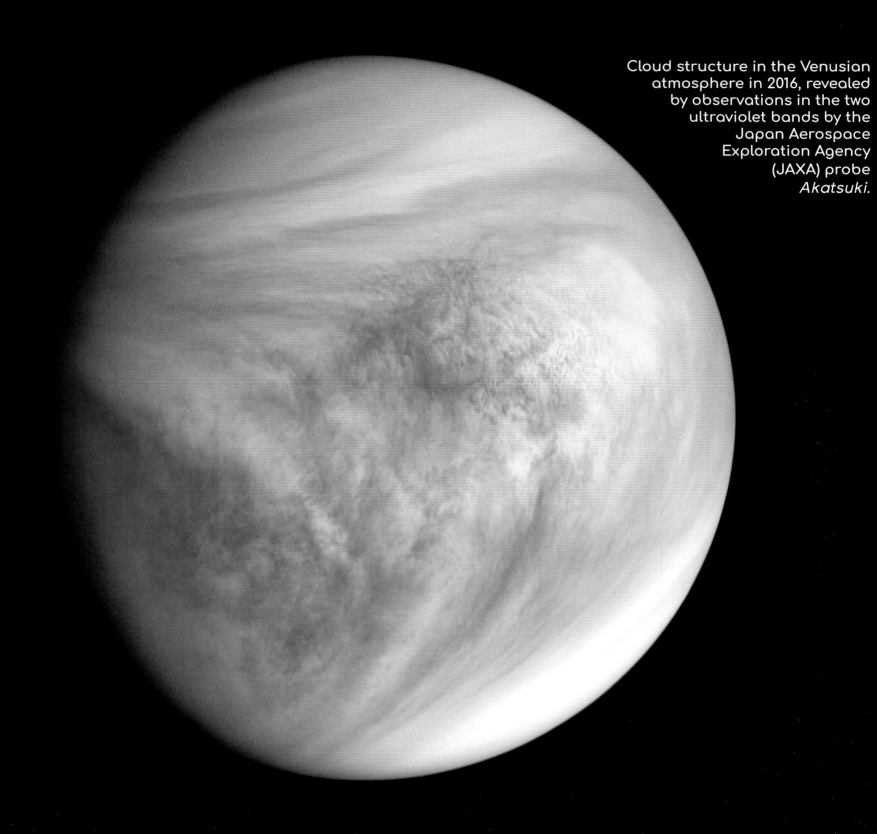

Cloud structure in the Venusian atmosphere in 2016, revealed by observations in the two ultraviolet bands by the Japan Aerospace Exploration Agency (JAXA) probe *Akatsuki*.

VENUS
12,100 km

EARTH
12,742 km

Atmosphere

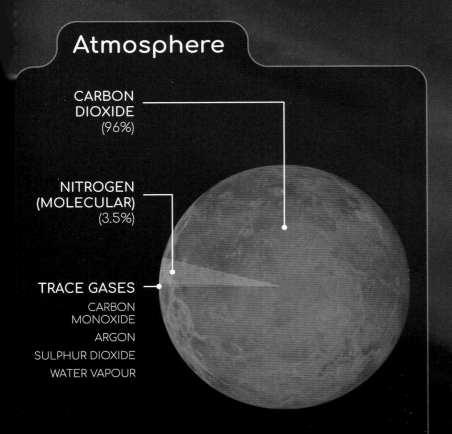

CARBON
DIOXIDE
(96%)

NITROGEN
(MOLECULAR)
(3.5%)

TRACE GASES
CARBON
MONOXIDE
ARGON
SULPHUR DIOXIDE
WATER VAPOUR

First recorded by humanity:	~1894 BCE
First recorded by:	Babylonian
Planet type:	Terrestrial
Distance from the Sun:	108.2 million km
Mass:	4.8673×10^{24} kg
Equatorial diameter:	12,100 km
Surface area:	460.2×10^6 km^2
Surface temperature range:	up to +480 °C
Gravity % compared to Earth:	90% (8.87 m/s^2)
Surface atmospheric pressure:	93 bar
Main atmosphere gases:	CO_2 (96%); N_2 (3%)
Number of moons:	None
Notable moons:	---
Number of rings:	None
Strength of magnetic field:	Weak
Direction of rotation:	East to West (2.6° tilt)
Rotational period (day length):	116 days 18 hrs
Orbital revolution (year length):	225 Earth days

The Solar System's Hottest Planet

Venus, named after the Roman goddess of love and beauty, is the second planet from the Sun and can be Earth's nearest neighbour, the shortest distance between the two being 61 million km.

It's the third brightest object in our sky after the Sun and the Moon. It's also about the same size and density as the Earth so the two have been called sisters or even twins, but they are really very different.

Venus has a thick, toxic atmosphere filled with carbon dioxide (96%) and it's perpetually shrouded in thick, yellowish clouds of sulphuric acid that trap heat. This creates an intense greenhouse effect - where a gaseous blanket is created in the upper atmosphere, allowing the Sun's radiation to penetrate but preventing the heat from this radiation to escape. The clouds also prevent its surface being seen from space (in visible light).

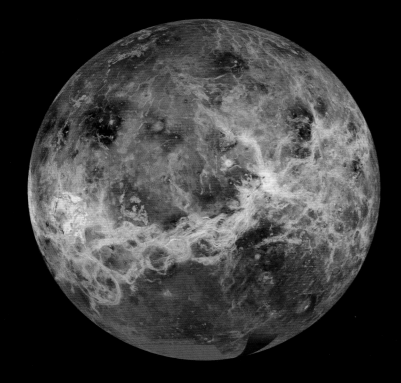

Venus (using a false-colour, radar-based image of the surface).

Impact craters on the surface of Venus (false-colour image reconstructed from radar data).

The self-heating which Venus undergoes makes it the hottest planet in our Solar System, even though Mercury is closer to the Sun. Surface temperatures on Venus average 462 °C, but can exceed 480 °C, which is hot enough to melt lead!

It also has crushing atmospheric pressure at its surface, about 92 times greater than being at sea level on Earth (or equivalent to being at 920 m depth beneath the sea's surface). It may be that the planet had watery oceans on it at some time in its very distant past, but these would have vapourised as the temperature rose due to the runaway greenhouse effect.

There is also almost no protective magnetic field originating from the core, so solar winds and intergalactic cosmic rays are continually bombarding it. This creates an induced magnetic field.

Internal Structure

It is presumed that, because they are of a similar size and density, Venus will have the same internal structure as Earth, but the data to support this are vague. It is believed that its core is of iron which is likely to be, at least partially, in a liquid state, but it may also be solid.

The mantle is of hot rock, while the crust is very thin and rocky. It would appear as though heat from the core is heating the crust, rather than driving a magnetic field. On occasion, volcanoes erupt through the crust in response to the ebb and flow of heat and pressure deep beneath.

Orbit and Rotation

The peculiarities about Venus continue if one looks at its rotation. The planet is the slowest spinner in the whole Solar System. As you know, Earth takes 24 hours to complete one full rotation and we call this time period a day. For one rotation of Venus, it takes 116 Earth days!

Another interesting (and rather disorientating) fact is that a Venus year (the time it takes to complete an orbit of the Sun) is shorter than its day length - 225 Earth days. Also, because Venus spins backwards (clockwise, if viewed above its north pole) when compared to Earth, sunrise happens in the west and sunset in the east.

Surface Features

It remains unclear as to why the surface of Venus is the way it is. It would appear that some 'resurfacing' work has been going on at some point in its past. Some believe this happened over the whole surface between 350 and 750 million years ago. Others think the resurfacing may have happened in a piecemeal fashion, with some parts being as young as 150 million years old.

Whatever its formative history, Venus is now a landscape of valleys and high mountains dotted with thousands of volcanoes, though with very few impact craters because only huge meteors can get through the atmosphere in tact. Some volcanoes have flat tops and have been nicknamed 'pancake' domes, while others have spurs radiating out from central points.

A model of *Venera 1*.

Magnetosphere

Whilst lacking a core-generated magnetic field, Venus has a much weaker, induced magnetic field. This is created by the interaction of the Sun's magnetic field and the planet's outer atmosphere. Ultraviolet radiation from the Sun excites gaseous molecules to become ions (thus forming an ionosphere). The solar wind of incredibly fast, charged particles carries with it the Sun's magnetic field which then interacts with the ionosphere, creating (or inducing) a magnetic field around Venus.

Below: 180-degree panorama of Venus's surface from the Soviet *Venera 9* lander, 1975. Black-and-white image of barren, black, slate-like rocks against a flat sky. The ground and the probe are the focus. Several lines are missing due to a simultaneous transmission of the scientific data.

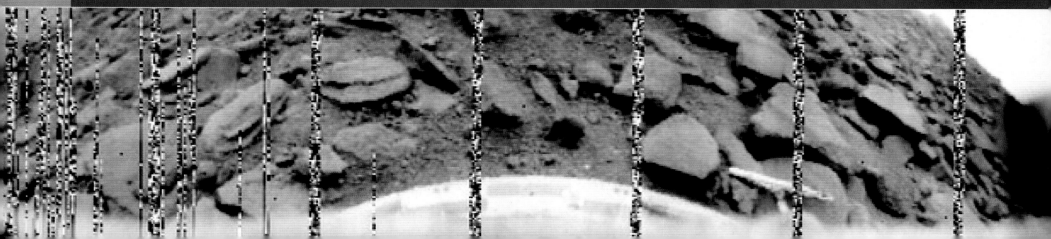

Missions to Venus

NASA's *Mariner 2* probe undertook a flyby of Venus on 14th December 1962 - the first robotic space probe to conduct a successful planetary encounter. Its purpose was to measure temperature variations on the planet's surface and to investigate its atmosphere.

The USSR launched 10 probes to explore Venus between 1967 and 1975, named the *Venera* missions. Sadly, only six of these missions were successful in sending back data. *Venera 7* was the first craft to land on another planet on 15th December 1970, although the last part of its descent was uncontrolled as its parachute only partially worked. The data sent back were limited, with transmissions lasting 53 minutes in total, 20 of which were from the surface. *Venera 8* had a successful touchdown on Venus some 16 months later. Remember, these were definitely one-way missions - the heat on touchdown would have been so hot as to melt the craft after about 20 minutes. In March 1982, *Venera 13* managed to send back the first sound recordings from another planet.

NASA's *Magellan* orbiter (1990-1994) mapped the surface of Venus over a four year period and also investigated its gravitational field. Further missions to Venus are being planned for the next two decades.

Astrobiology

About 50 km above the surface of Venus, the temperature drops to 30-70 °C. Theoretically, this is within the range of microbes capable of tolerating extremes. There are dark streaks which appear above the clouds at this altitude and some scientists think these streaks could be made up of microbial life.

Below: Photo of the surface of Venus taken by the *Venera 13* lander on March 1, 1982.

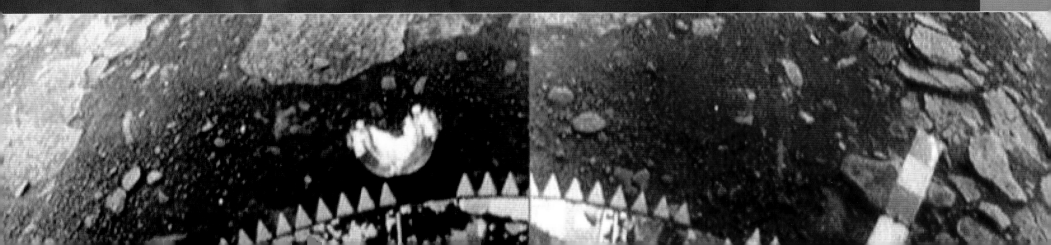

EARTH

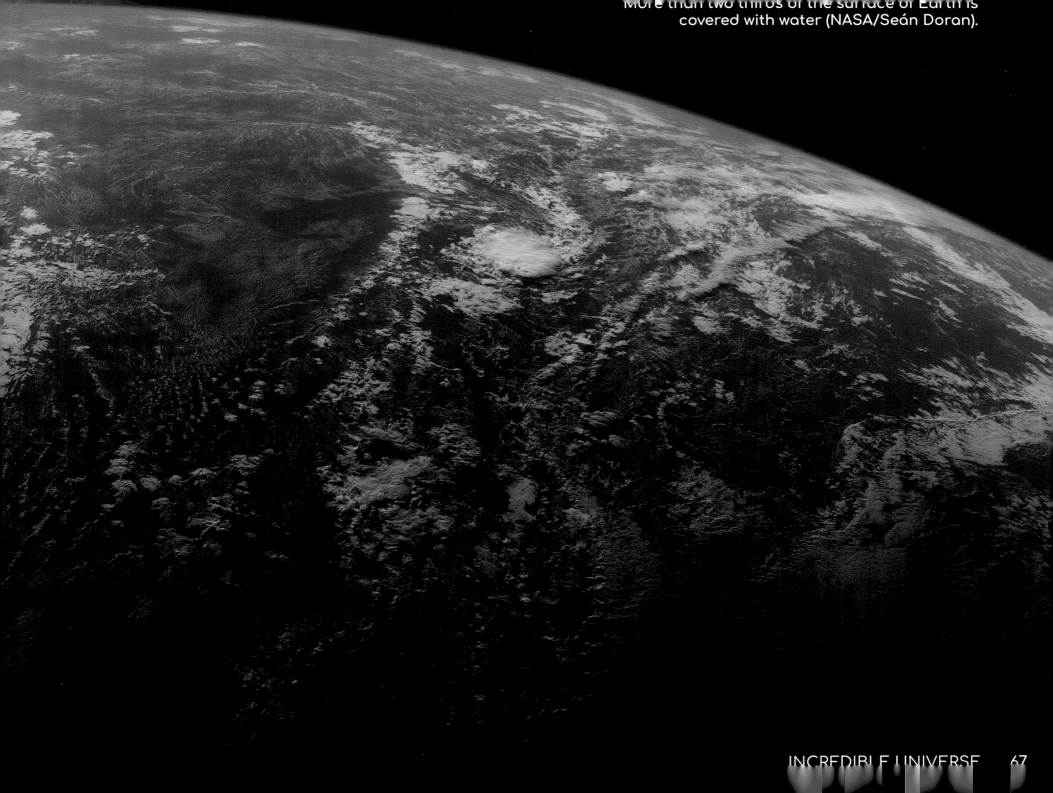

This photo, called 'The Blue Marble', is the most widely used photograph of Earth. It was taken by the *Apollo 17* mission in 1972.

How Big?
Equatorial Diameters

THE MOON
3,475 km

EARTH
12,742 km

Atmosphere

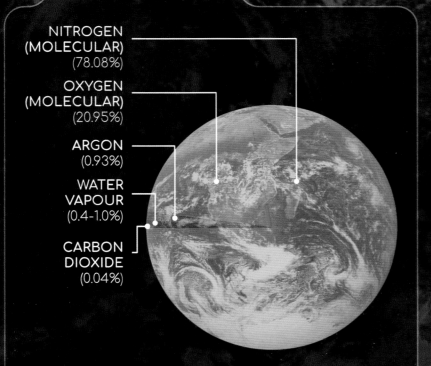

NITROGEN
(MOLECULAR)
(78.08%)

OXYGEN
(MOLECULAR)
(20.95%)

ARGON
(0.93%)

WATER
VAPOUR
(0.4-1.0%)

CARBON
DIOXIDE
(0.04%)

Key Facts

First recorded by humanity:	---
First recorded by:	---
Planet type:	**Terrestrial**
Distance from the Sun:	**149.6 million km**
Mass:	**5.972×10^{24} kg**
Equatorial diameter:	**12,742 km**
Surface area:	**510.1×10^{6} km^2**
Surface temperature range:	**-88 °C to +58 °C**
Gravity % compared to Earth:	**9.807 m/s^2**
Surface atmospheric pressure:	**1 bar**
Main atmosphere gases:	**N_2 (78%); O_2 (21%)**
Number of moons:	**1**
Notable moons:	**The Moon**
Number of rings:	**None**
Strength of magnetic field:	**Strong**
Direction of rotation:	**West to East (23° tilt)**
Rotational period (day length):	**24 hrs 0 mins**
Orbital revolution (year length):	**365.25 Earth days**

Our Home

We live on the third planet from the Sun and, as far as we currently know, this is the only planet where life is known to exist within our Solar System.

Out of the eight planets within our Solar System, Earth is the fifth largest and the only one where water is present on the surface in a liquid state. In fact, water covers about 71% of the Earth's surface, and as it looks mostly blue and white from space, many think our home should be called 'Planet Ocean'.

While all of the other planets in our Solar System have been named after Greek and Roman gods and godesses, the name 'Earth' actually derives from a German word meaning 'the ground'.

The average distance of the Earth from the Sun is about 150 million km (93 million miles). It takes about 8 mins. 20 secs. for light to travel this distance which means that, when we look at the Sun, or any other object that is lit by the Sun's light, we are actually looking into the past. It takes the Earth 365.25 days to complete its elliptical orbit around the Sun.

Earth has an axial tilt of 23.4°, meaning that instead of spinning on an upright north-south axis, this axis is tilted so that the north pole leans towards the Sun for part of its orbit and away from the Sun for the other part. This orientation creates the seasons, experienced by those living in the higher latitudes of both the northern and southern hemispheres (albeit at opposite times), and why there is a lack of similar seasons in a narrow band either side of the Equator.

Internal Structure and Atmosphere

Similar to the other terrestrial planets of Mercury, Venus and Mars, Earth consists of an inner core, an outer core, a mantle and a crust.

The inner core consists of iron (Fe) and nickel (Ni) metals at a temperature of 5,400 °C. The outer core is also composed of iron and nickel in a fluid state. The mantle is the thickest layer. It consists of a hot mixture of molten rock with the consistency of caramel. The crust has an average thickness of about 30 km over land, but under the oceans it thins to about 5 km thickness.

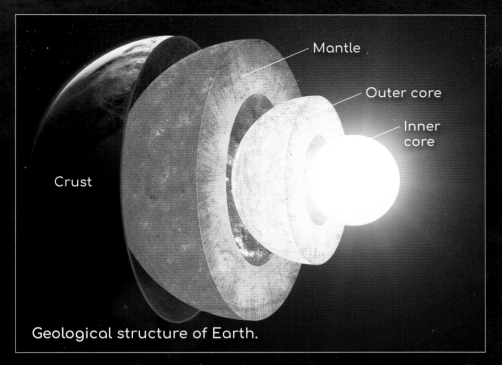

Mantle

Outer core

Inner core

Crust

Geological structure of Earth.

The crust and the upper mantle (known together as the lithosphere) are divided into tectonic plates. These are constantly moving, albeit at a very slow speed, equivalent to the growth of our fingernails.

Earthquakes result when the plates grind past one another or ride up over each other. They may also collide to make mountains (as happened in the formation of the Himalayas), or split and separate (as is happening along the Mid-Atlantic Ridge).

The iron-rich core of Earth generates the planet's magnetic field, causing compasses to point to the North Pole, regardless of which way you turn.

The magnetism of Earth generates a magnetosphere around our planet which deflects much of the ionised particles in the solar wind, although some may collide with air molecules above the poles, creating spectacular light displays which we know as the Northern and Southern Lights.

Earth's atmosphere shields us from the harmful radiation coming from the Sun. It also protects us from meteoroids, most of which burn up in the atmosphere (seen as meteors in the night sky), before they can strike the surface as meteorites.

The atmosphere also plays an essential role in maintaining hospitable and (relatively) stable temperatures across Earth's surface. Much of the Sun's heat passes through the atmosphere, but is reflected from the surface and become trapped by gases in the upper atmosphere. This process both raises the average temperature of the planet and moderates the extremes in temperature fluctuation.

Planets and Moons that largely lack an atmosphere can be subject to massive temperature variation which may vary more than 300°C between sunlit areas and shade (such as the Moon, see page 73).

Our Moon

Earth has just one moon, which our forebears named the Moon. No other moons were known until Galileo Galilei discovered four moons orbiting Jupiter in 1610. Ours is the fifth largest moon in the Solar System. The average distance between it and Earth is about 384,400 km. The Moon's size and its distance from Earth leads to a gravitational tension between the two, moderating the wobble which the Earth creates as it spins around its axis. The presence of the Moon also generates tides in Earth's oceans which, depending on the direction of pull, can either be large (spring tides) or weak (neap tides).

The Moon was probably created when an object the size of Mars collided with the Earth during its early history. It rotates at the same rate that it revolves around Earth (called synchronous rotation), so the same hemisphere faces Earth all the time. Some people call the far side – the hemisphere we never see from Earth – the 'dark side' but that's rather misleading as it is lit by the Sun at times when we experience a 'new' moon (as opposed to a full moon).

There's little atmosphere on the Moon, so there is no barrier to prevent impacts from meteoroids and comets. The number of impact craters apparent on the Moon's surface is testament to this bombardment. Nearly the entire surface is covered by the debris of these impacts, particularly of powdery dust and small rocks termed 'lunar regolith'.

The lighter areas of the Moon (as seen from Earth) are known as *Highlands* and the darker areas as *Maria* (Latin for seas). They indicate rocks of different ages and composition. If you've seen any film of when the *Apollo* astronauts landed on the Moon (between 1969 and 1972), you'll have noticed how they 'bounced' over the surface. This is because the Moon's gravity is just one-sixth of Earth's.

The temperature on the surface of the Moon in full sunlight rises to 127 °C, but in shade, the surface can fall to -173 °C. This is because the Moon lacks an atmosphere which otherwise may regulate its temperature. In September 2021, NASA announced plans to send a robotic rover to look for water-ice close to the Moon's south pole in the next few years. Should water-ice be found, it could be later mined for use as drinking water or as rocket fuel (by splitting the H_2O molecules into oxygen and hydrogen). If all goes well, NASA aims to return astronauts to the Moon by the end of the 2020 decade.

The surface temperature of the moon fluctuates greatly between areas in sunlight and shadow.

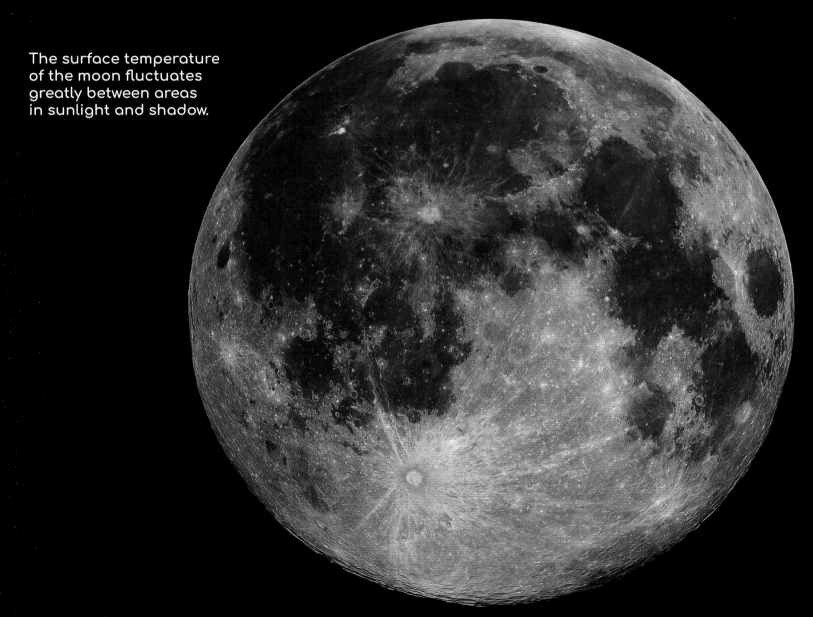

How did Life Start on Earth?

Earth is thought to have formed, along with all the other planets in the Solar System, about 4.5 billion years ago. It was totally lifeless for about a further one billion years, after which simple microorganisms began to appear. How did this come about? The simple answer is that scientists are still not sure, but various theories have been proposed.

We know that life on Earth is built of compounds that contain elements such as carbon (C), nitrogen (N), hydrogen (H) and oxygen (O). Complex sequences of these elements bond together, forming the very building blocks of life. They form essential organic molecules, such as sugars, enzymes, proteins and DNA. However, these organic molecules did not naturally exist on Earth when the first origins of life appeared. The elements required existed only in inorganic form, bound up within the rocks, atmosphere and the early ocean.

During the 1950s, laboratory experiments were undertaken whereby such inorganic molecules containing these elements were mixed together with water, gases and exposed to electrical sparks mimicking lightning (see the Miller–Urey experiment on page 24). These experiments created simple organic molecules known as amino acids, which are the building blocks of proteins, the progenitors of life.

Were these conditions the same to what might have existed 3.5 billion years ago? Some scientists now say that the energy source would have been inadequate to produce lifeforms capable of reproducing. With similar ingredients, they propose that the energy source would have been a 'natural nuclear reactor' deep within the Earth's core, something that no longer exists on Earth today. It may be some time yet before agreement is reached as to exactly how it all started. One thing is for sure though: our present existence has only come about through the process of evolution over an incredibly long time.

Our planet is within what has been termed 'the Goldilocks zone' around our star, the Sun. The term indicates the fact that the location of Earth from the Sun means it's not too hot and it's not too cold for life to exist here - it's just right.

This position allows for water, regarded as a 'must have' ingredient for life (as we know it), to be present as a liquid (although in the colder parts of our planet it freezes and becomes ice).

In 2013, astronomers calculated that there could be as many as 11 billion Earth-sized planets orbiting Sun-like stars within our Galaxy, the Milky Way, and which lie within their own 'Goldilocks zone'. Remember, the Observable Universe may contain more than 2 trillion other galaxies (see page 19), so, it may be reasonable to think that on one of those planets, some form of life might have evolved. But if so, a serious question is raised: where are the aliens? See the Fermi Paradox, page 23.

Astrobiologists have focused on studying 'extremophiles'; forms of life on Earth that can exist in extreme environments.

An important group of extremophiles are life forms that live around hydrothermal vents (known as 'black smokers') on the ocean floor.

These fissures within the seabed release super-heated water, and around these vents are communities of animals that exist via chemosynthesis instead of photosythesis. They derive energy from chemicals released from the vents, rather than sunlight, and in some cases, have complex foodwebs.

These sorts of conditions have now been found on planets and moons beyond the goldilocks zone of our Solar System, so it is in these places that scientists hold out the most hope of finding signs of life.

MARS

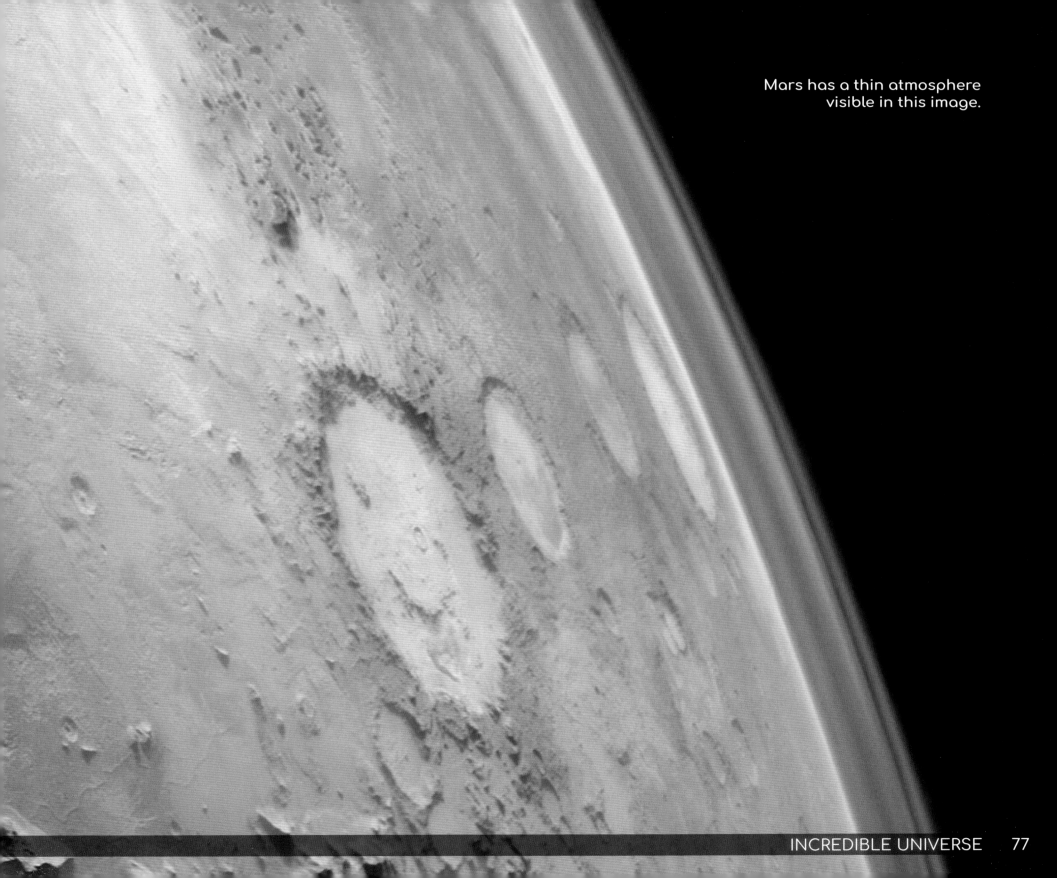

Mars has a thin atmosphere
visible in this image.

MARS
6,779 km

EARTH
12,742 km

Atmosphere

CARBON DIOXIDE
(96%)

NITROGEN
(1.9%)

ARGON
(1.9%)

TRACE GASES
ACETYLENE
CARBON MONOXIDE
KRYPTON
METHANE
NEON
NITROGEN OXIDE
OXYGEN
OZONE
WATER VAPOUR
XENON

First recorded by humanity:	**2nd millennium BCE**
First recorded by:	**Egyptians**
Planet type:	**Terrestrial**
Distance from the Sun:	**227.9 million km**
Mass:	**0.639×10^{24} kg**
Equatorial diameter:	**6,779 km**
Surface area:	**144.8×10^6 km^2**
Surface temperature range:	**-153 °C to +20 °C**
Gravity % compared to Earth:	**38% (3.721 m/s^2)**
Surface atmospheric pressure:	**0.01 bar**
Main atmosphere gases:	**CO_2 (95%); N_2 (3%)**
Number of moons:	**2**
Notable moons:	**Phobos; Deimos**
Number of rings:	**None**
Strength of magnetic field:	**Very weak**
Direction of rotation:	**West to East (25.2° tilt)**
Rotational period (day length):	**24 hrs 37 mins**
Orbital revolution (year length):	**687 Earth days**

The cold, dusty landscape of Mars.

The Red Planet

Mars is the fourth planet from the Sun. It lies an average of 246.31 million km from the Sun, although it follows an elliptical orbit so the distance varies over time. Mars is about half the size of Earth.

Mars was named by the Romans after their god of war, because its reddish colour is reminiscent of blood. Today it is often referred to as the red planet, as its soils are high in iron oxide which has a rusty red colour. It is one of five planets that can be seen with the naked eye in the night sky, though the only one which has a reddish colour to it.

Mars was first viewed using a telescope in 1610 by the Italian astronomer Galileo Galilei. As the quality of telescopes improved, so did the descriptions of Mars and of its position in space. The two polar ice caps, both coloured white, were soon described along with a variety of surface features whose exact nature could only be guessed at. Jump forward in time and the Hubble Space Telescope has revealed many of Mars's secrets in incredible detail.

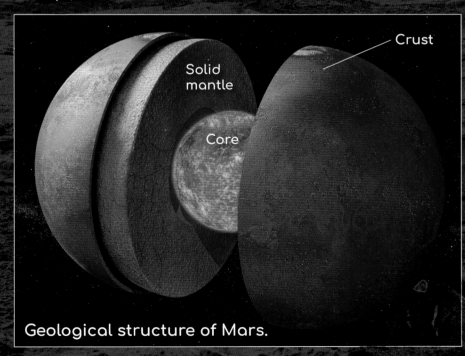

Geological structure of Mars.

Mars has featured heavily in the minds of science fiction writers over the years. One of the most famous stories was written by H. G. Wells in 1898 entitled *The War of the Worlds*. It featured an attack on the Earth by a warmongering Martian race.

A play based on the book was broadcast on American radio in 1938 and it was so real that thousands of listeners believed they were really being attacked by aliens!

During the late 19th and early 20th centuries, many astronomers incorrectly believed that they could see 'canals' on the planet Mars and regarded these as real evidence of Marian civilisations. We now know the canals to be an optical illusion.

Internal Structure and Atmosphere

Like Earth, Mars is a terrestrial planet, possessing a dense, metallic inner core, an overlying silicate mantle and an outer crust with an average thickness of 50 km. Mars has been found to be seismically active, with 'marsquakes' regularly recorded. In fact, during 2019, over 450 of these were detected.

As a result of its core cooling and partially solidifying, Mars has lost its ability to generate a magnetic field (magnetosphere) about 4 billion years ago, possibly the result of numerous asteroid strikes. This means that much of its atmosphere has been stripped away by solar winds.

A trail of ionised particles departing Mars has been detected by orbiting spacecraft and is due to be studied in detail by the *MAVEN* orbiter. Consequently, Mars has a thin atmosphere creating a very low surface atmospheric pressure.

Earth's inner core is very hot but solid. Its outer core remains in a liquid state and because it rotates, the two act like a dynamo, creating electromagnetic energy and generating a magnetic field around the planet. Whilst Mars would have had a magnetic field early in the planet's life, its core has since cooled and solidified, resulting in most of its magnetic field being lost. This has had a big effect on its atmosphere.

Mars is dry, rocky and bitterly cold. Its atmosphere consists of about 96% carbon dioxide (CO_2), 1.93% argon (Ar) and 1.89% nitrogen (N_2) along with traces of oxygen (O_2) and water (H_2O). When viewed from the planet's surface, the Martian sky takes on a tawny colour due to suspended fine particles, whipped up by periodic dust storms.

Surface Features

The surface of Mars is peppered not only with impact craters of all sizes but also with many impressive features. Take *Valles Marineris* for example. This large canyon system is 4,800 km long, 320 km at its widest and it descends 7 km deep! Mars is also home to *Olympus Mons*, the largest volcano in the Solar System (though no longer active). It's three times taller then Mount Everest!

The north and south hemispheres of Mars appear quite different. Much of the north is smooth and of low elevation. By contrast, the southern half is rough with a great number of craters, indicating an older age. It's been proposed that the northern part may have been impacted by a large planetary body early on in Mars's life.

The ice cap in the north is much larger than the one in the south. It consists of a large pattern of spirally-arranged troughs. The total volume of water-ice here is estimated to be 821,000 km^3.

Various probes have also detected water ice below the planet's surface, as well as sub-glacial lakes. Should all of these water sources be melted, enough liquid water would be released to flood Mars to a depth of between 5 - 10 m (if spread evenly around the planet's surface). If this happened though, Mars would not be covered by a global ocean, as most of the water would coalesce in depressions and low-lying areas such as the *Hellas Planitia* (8 kilometers deep!).

Recent discoveries prove that Mars did have a watery past, with ancient river valley networks, deltas, and lakebeds, as well as rocks and minerals on the surface that could only have formed in liquid water.

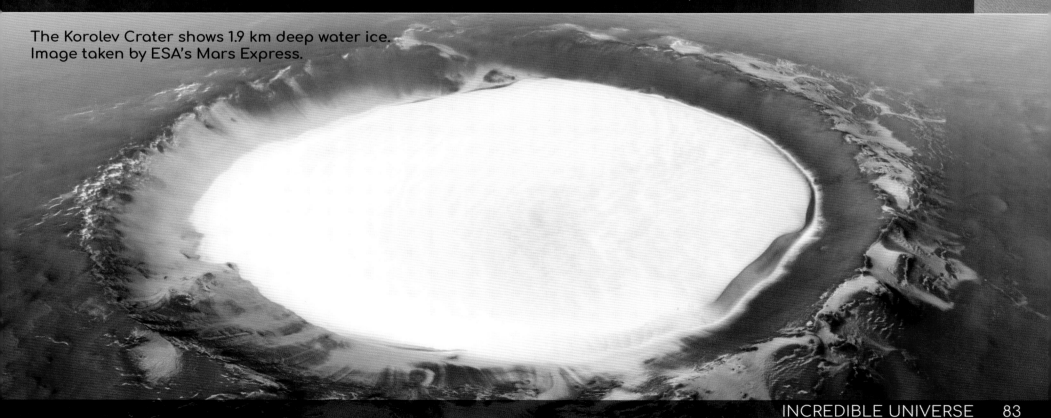

The Korolev Crater shows 1.9 km deep water ice.
Image taken by ESA's Mars Express.

The Naming of Mars's features

The Italian astronomer Giovanni Schiaparelli drew a map of Mars in 1886 and named many of the large, obvious features in Italian although using names from Greek mythology and, on occasion, the bible.

Examples include *Hellas Planitia* ('the plain of Greece'), which is also the lowest area on the planet; or *Elysium Mons* ('the mountain of heaven'), one of the highest parts.

Many more features have now been given names from a variety of sources. For example, large craters are named after important scientists and science fiction writers, while smaller ones are named after towns and villages on Earth.

Mars's Moons

Two moons orbit around Mars: Phobos and Deimos. However, their small size means they are potato-shaped and not spherical. It's possible they are both 'captured asteroids', meaning asteroids which are held by Mars's gravitational force.

The moons get their names from the horses that pulled the chariot of the Greek god of war, Ares.

Phobos, the innermost and larger moon, is heavily cratered, with deep grooves on its surface. It is slowly moving towards Mars and will crash into the planet or break apart in about 50 million years.

Deimos is about half as big as Phobos and orbits two and a half times farther away from Mars. Oddly-shaped Deimos is covered in loose dirt that often fills the craters on its surface, making it appear smoother than pockmarked Phobos.

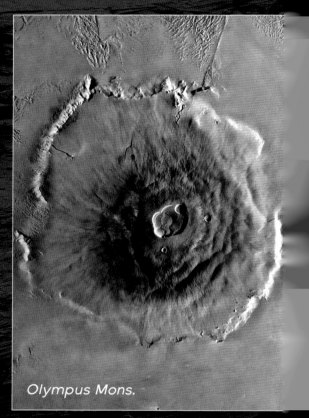

Olympus Mons.

Valles Marineris.

Missions to Mars

Mars is one of the most explored bodies in our Solar System - we have been sending robotic spacecraft there since the 1960s. Not only have spacecraft been in orbit around it, it's the only planet that has been explored by rovers too. As this book is being written, NASA has two rovers (*Curiosity* and *Perseverance*), one lander (*InSight*) and one mini-helicopter (*Ingenuity*) exploring the surface of Mars.

Craft from other nations are also exploring Mars during 2021. China's *Tianwen-1* mission arrived in February 2021 and included an orbiter, a lander and a rover. Its *Zhourong* rover landed on Mars in May 2021. And in February 2021, the *Hope* orbiter arrived from the United Arab Emirates. This makes up an international fleet of eight orbiters that are currently circumnavigating the Red Planet, including three from NASA: *2001 Mars Odyssey*, *Mars Reconnaissance Orbiter* and *MAVEN*.

This rush of craft heading to Mars was no coincidence. They were all making the most of a 'window of opportunity'. Mars launches are scheduled when Earth and Mars are closest to each other, allowing mission planners to minimise the rocket energy required and to maximise the weight of their spacecraft. It takes almost twice as long for Mars to orbit the Sun than Earth — 365 days versus 687 days — which means Earth and Mars will be at their closest roughly every 2 years.

Many other missions to Mars are being planned for the coming years. One that is certain to happen will be a joint NASA/ESA series of missions named Mars Sample Return. These will return soil and rock samples (collected in tubes by the *Perseverance* rover) to Earth, firstly using mini-rockets to blast the samples to a craft orbiting Mars, and then sending them on to Earth for eventual scientific analysis.

The possibility of humans living in colonies on Mars is no longer the stuff of science fiction, but is very much a reality and may even happen within your lifetime - see the *Exploring Mars* chapter.

Astrobiology

Mars is regarded as one of the Solar System's best candidates for life beyond Earth, either extant (living underground, in lava tubes or caves, perhaps where geothermal activity melts sub-surface ice) or fossilised (from earlier times when liquid water would have flowed across the Martian surface).

THE ASTEROID BELT

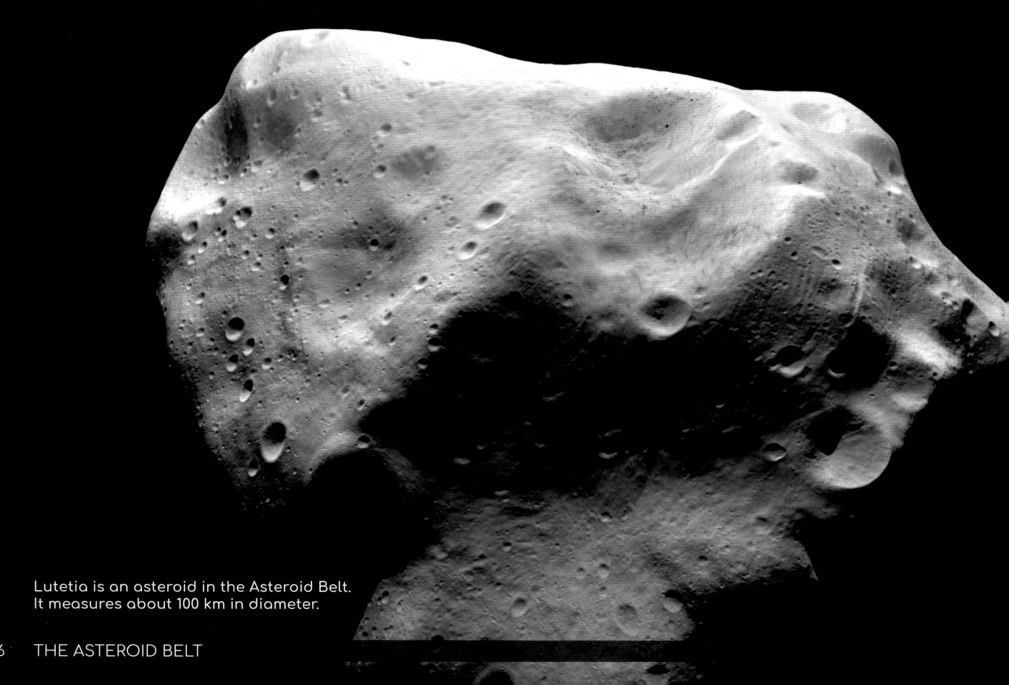

Lutetia is an asteroid in the Asteroid Belt.
It measures about 100 km in diameter.

The Asteroid Belt is a ring of asteroids located between the orbits of Jupiter and Mars. Asteroids are remnants left over from the early formation of our Solar System about 4.6 billion years ago.

Currently, over 1.1 million asteroids are known to make up the belt, but astronomers think the total number may be far greater.

Detected asteroids range in size from less than 10 m across, to giants such as Vesta (530 km long, see background image of this page), Pallas and Hygiea (both around 400 km long). Within the Asteroid Belt is the dwarf planet Ceres (950 km) in diameter. Ceres is round, yet is considered too small to be a full-fledged planet. The total mass of all the asteroids combined is less than that of Earth's Moon.

Most asteroids are irregularly shaped and largely made of rock, although a minority contain iron and nickel metals. Some of the more distant asteroids contain ice. Asteroids aren't large enough to maintain an atmosphere. No asteroids are thought to support any possibilities for life as we know it.

The Asteroid Belt is also called the 'Main Asteroid Belt' or 'Main Belt' to distinguish it from other asteroid populations in the Solar System such as near-Earth asteroids and trojan asteroids.

Asteroids of the inner Solar System.

The asteroid Ida and its moon Dacty.

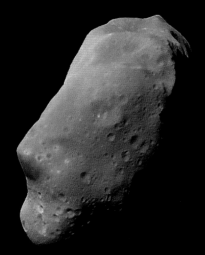

JUPITER

Storms rage across Jupiter's surface (NASA/Seán Doran).

Jupiter is the biggest planet
in our Solar System.

How Big?
Equatorial Diameters

JUPITER
139,822 km

EARTH
12,742 km

Atmosphere

HYDROGEN
(MOLECULAR)
(~90%)

HELIUM
(MONATOMIC)
(~10%)

TRACE
AMOUNTS
METHANE
AMMONIA
HYDROGEN
SULPHIDE
WATER VAPOUR
PHOSPHINE

Key Facts

First recorded by humanity:	**8th century BCE**
First recorded by:	**Babylonians**
Planet type:	**Gas giant**
Distance from the Sun:	**778.6 million km**
Mass:	**$1,898 \times 10^{24}$ kg**
Equatorial diameter:	**139,822 km**
Surface area:	**61.42×10^{9} km^2**
Surface temperature range:	**down to -100 °C**
Gravity % compared to Earth:	**253% (24.79 m/s^2)**
Surface atmospheric pressure:	**>1,000 bar**
Main atmosphere gases:	**H_2 (90%); He (10%)**
Number of moons:	**at least 75**
Notable moons:	**Io; Europa; Callisto**
Number of rings:	**Faint rings present**
Strength of magnetic field:	**Very strong**
Direction of rotation:	**West to East (3° tilt)**
Rotational period (day length):	**9 hrs 56 mins**
Orbital revolution (year length):	**4,333 Earth days**

The Solar System's Giant!

Jupiter is the fifth planet from the Sun and the largest planet in the Solar System. To provide some idea of how large Jupiter is, the planet's mass is more than two and a half times the mass of all the other planets in the Solar System combined. It is still dwarfed by the Sun however, which has a mass over 1,000 times greater. At its equator, Jupiter has a diameter of 142,984 km (88,846 miles) - Earth's diameter at its equator is 12,742 km.

Jupiter is a gas giant composed mainly of hydrogen and helium, although it is suspected of having a rocky core of heavier elements. It is one of two gas giants in our Solar System, the other being its neighbour Saturn.

Because the Sun, our star, is also mostly composed of these gases, these two planets are sometimes referred to as being 'failed stars'. That means, because they are not sufficiently massive to have the internal pressure and temperature necessary to cause hydrogen to fuse to helium, they are unable to produce the energy that the Sun does.

However, the on-going contraction of Jupiter's interior generates more heat than the amount it receives from the Sun.

Jupiter's orbit maintains a distance of approximately 778.5 million km from the Sun. It completes one orbit around the Sun (in effect, a Jupiter year) in the same time it takes the Earth to complete 11.86 orbits. It also boasts the fastest spin of a planet in our Solar System, completing one revolution is just under 10 hours (it takes Earth, of course, 24 hours to do this).

Those planning missions to Jupiter have to allow for the spacecraft to take 6-7 years to reach the planet.

Jupiter is the third brightest object in our night sky, with only the Moon and Venus being brighter. It is named after the Roman god Jupiter, the king of the gods, because of its large size.

Jupiter's Atmosphere

Jupiter's atmosphere is the deepest known in the Solar System, spanning at least 5,000 km in altitude. It consists of a continuously swirling mass of clouds, possibly made up of ammonium hydrosulphide. Interactions between conflicting circulation patterns cause storms and turbulence. Wind speeds of up to 100 metres per second are common in what are known as zonal jet streams.

The cloud layer is about 50 km deep. There may also be a thin layer of water clouds underlying the ammonia layer. The water clouds are believed to generate thunderstorms, as flashes of lightning have been observed from time to time, measured as being 1,000 times as powerful as lightning on Earth. These storms seem to be never-ending.

The orange and brown colours in Jupiter's clouds are caused by upwelling compounds that change colour when they are exposed to ultraviolet light from the Sun. It's thought that phosphorus, sulphur or hydrocarbons may be responsible for these colours.

The Great Red Spot

Located 22° to the south of Jupiter's equator, the Great Red Spot is the name given to a persistent storm, with winds circulating in an counter-clockwise direction.

It is oval in shape and takes about six Earth-days to complete one revolution. Nobody knows for sure why it's a red colour, but it may be due to the light-affected ammonia molecules reacting with acetylene molecules.

The Spot itself is so big that the Earth could fit inside it! When first measured at the end of the 1800s, its longest dimension was 41,000 km, and it was thought to be a permanent feature.

However, with subsequent measurements that have been taken by the Hubble telescope and by fly-by spacecraft, it is reducing in size by about 930 km each year. In 2015, it was approximately 16,500 km long.

One wonders what will have happened to it by the mid-2040s?

Other vortices have also been discovered around Jupiter's north and south poles, known as 'polar cyclones', which typically appear as groups.

The group at the north pole consists of a large, central cyclone surrounded by eight smaller ones. These are thought to occur because of turbulence in the atmosphere in these regions, likely to be associated with temperature changes.

Jupiter's Great Red Spot.

The Great Red Spot is larger than Earth (NASA/Seán Doran).

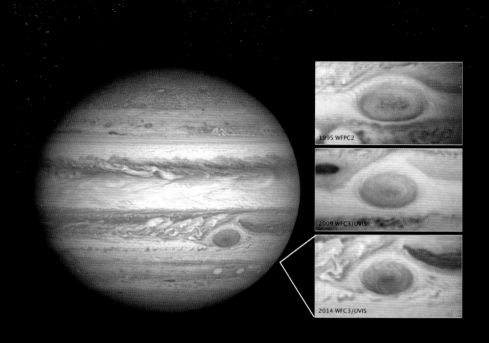

The Great Red Spot is decreasing in size (upper photo 1995, middle photo 2009, lower photo 2014).

Aurorae on the North Pole (Hubble).

The tempestuous atmosphere of Jupiter, captured by the Wide Field Camera 3 on the Hubble Space Telescope in infrared.

Ultraviolet view of Jupiter (Hubble).

79 Moons and Counting?

Astronomers believe Jupiter has as many as 79 moons, though there may be still more out there waiting to be discovered. At present there are 53 named moons and another 26 still awaiting names.

Those moons of greatest interest have been the first four of Jupiter's that were discovered, known as the Gallilean satellites: Io, Europa, Ganymede and Callisto. They were discovered in 1610 by Galileo Galilei, the Italian scientist who developed the newly invented telescope to look at the night sky. His telescope at the time could enlarge an image 20 times. These four moons also happen to be the planet's largest.

Each of these moons is quite distinctive. Io (named after a priestess from Greek mythology) is the innermost and third largest of the four Galilean moons. It is slightly larger than our own moon. With over 400 active volcanoes, Io is the most geologically active object in the Solar System. This due to the heat that's generated from gravitational forces from Jupiter and the other three Galilean moons. Plumes of sulphur from exploding volcanoes can extend 500 km above the surface, and these have painted the surface in a multitude of colours. There's no sign of any water on Io; in fact it's the driest place in the whole Solar System, being formed almost entirely of silicate rock.

The Galilean moons of Jupiter.

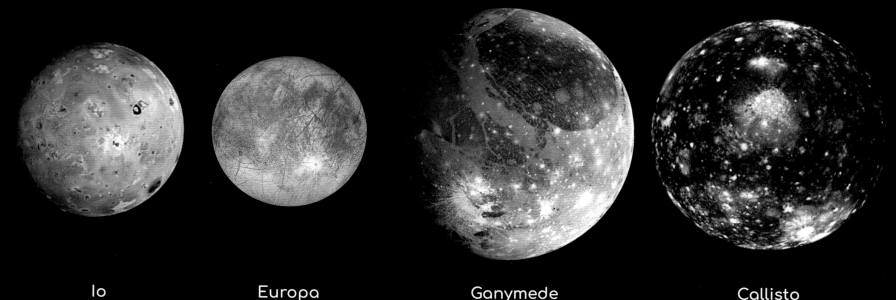

Io   Europa   Ganymede   Callisto

Europa is the smallest of the Gailiean moons and it's just a little smaller than our own moon. Described as 'one of the most beautiful moons in the entire Solar System', it's made of silicate rock with a crust of water-ice and a core of nickel-iron. Its surface isn't pock-marked with craters but instead, strangely, it is striated with cracks and fractures, correctly called 'lineae'. These mark weak parts of the ice crust, created by 'tidal' forces generated between Europa and Jupiter. It has a very thin atmosphere, primarily composed of oxygen.

The smooth nature of the Europa's surface is thought to indicate the surface is constantly reforming, perhaps with new material being brought up to the surface from deeper down. The smooth surface, the smoothest of any known celestial object in the Solar System, is indicative of a watery ocean lying beneath. Scientists believe there's a strong possibility of finding extra-terrestrial life within this ocean. This is investigated further under 'Astrobiology'.

Ganymede is the largest moon present in the Solar System. It has a diameter of 5,268 km, which makes it bigger than the planet Mercury. Ganymede is composed of approximately equal parts of silicate rock and water. It has an iron-rich, liquid core, leading to it being the only moon in the Solar System to have its own magnetic field. Between the core and the outer crust there is an internal ocean that may contain

Two possible models of Europa

Metallic Core

Cold Brittle Surface Ice

Rocky Interior

H_2O Layer

Warm Convecting Ice

Metallic Core

Ice Covering

Rocky Interior

H_2O Layer

Liquid Ocean Under Ice

Enhanced-colour view showing the intricate pattern of linear fractures on Europa's surface

more water than all of Earth's oceans combined. About a third of the moon's surface is covered by dark regions with many impact craters; and the remaining two thirds are lighter, being cross-cut by extensive grooves and ridges. It's not clear why or how this division has come about.

Callisto is Jupiter's second largest moon and the third largest moon in the Solar System (after Ganymede and Saturn's Titan). Callisto is also the outermost of the four Galilean moons. Its surface is the most heavily cratered in the Solar System. It is composed of approximately equal quantities of rock and ice. Below its surface is thought to be a salty ocean and consequently it may harbour life there too.

Might There be Life on Europa?

In the past few years, a large amount of attention has been directed at the moon Europa and the possibility of life existing there. Although it's not found within the 'Goldilocks zone' around our Sun (that is, at a distance from the Sun which provides just the right temperature on the surface for life to survive), there's enough evidence to think there could well be some form of life there.

In 2012, at the south pole on Europa, erupting plumes of water vapour as high as 200 km were observed by the Hubble telescope. This observation supports the view that water is present below the crust.

A hydrothermal vent in the Atlantic Ocean. Could similar vents occur in Europa's sub-surace seas? Could they support life?

An artist's impression of a future mission to explore Europa's sub-surface seas.

The icy surface of Europa.

Interestingly, it's also been proposed that the crust is not attached to any rocky part of Europa, meaning that it floats and rotates as a whole in a way that's different to the moon itself.

The sub-surface ocean on Europa is thought to be more than 10 times as deep as any on Earth, and to contain twice as much water by volume. It's also believed that this water has been there since the birth of the Solar System, hidden beneath the moon's icy surface. 'So why is it not all ice?', you may ask.

Well, the tidal movement of the moon's core, which is caused by the push-and-pull of its elliptical orbit around Jupiter, creates energy in the form of heat.

This heat keeps the water in a liquid state. It's also thought it may give rise to hydrothermal vents (where hot gases are continuously released from geothermal activity) occurring on the floor of the ocean.

Io is the innermost and third-largest of Jupiter's our Galilean moons.

Being 780 million km away from the Sun, Europa receives 25 times less sunlight than the Earth. As a result, it's very cold - temperatures on the surface have been measured at -160 °C at the equator and -220 °C at the poles. However, as it's believed there's liquid water beneath the 15-25 km thick water-ice crust, the temperature here must be above 0 °C.

Europa would appear to have the three elements required for life: water, minerals and energy. The strong likelihood of hydrothermal vents helping to heat the water could well mean there are lifeforms existing around these vents, possibly similar to those which have been found in the ocean depths on Earth, far from the Sun's light.

Within the next 15-20 years, we should be able to answer the question: Does Europa sustain life? How exciting is that!

Missions to Jupiter

When the Earth and Jupiter are at the closest point in their elliptical orbits (a position known as 'perihelion'), they are 588 million km (365 million miles) apart. At the furthest extent of their orbits ('aphelion'), they may be 968 million km apart. So, in order to minimise the journeying time, the launch of a spacecraft is timed to coincide with the minimum distance between the two. Even so, it may still take between two years (*Voyager 1*) and over six years (*Galileo*). This is partly because of the need to 'slingshot' around other planets and moons in order to save fuel and increase the speed of the craft.

There have been nine spacecraft which have returned information about Jupiter and its moons back to Earth. All of these have been NASA missions. Most of these have been as fly-by missions, meaning that Jupiter was encountered while the craft were on their way to other planets. The nine in question have been *Pioneer 10* (1973), *Pioneer 11* (1974), *Voyagers 1* & *2* (1979), *Ulysses* (1992 & 2000), *Cassini* (2000), *New Horizons* (2007), *Galileo* (1995-2003) and *Juno* (2016). The *Juno* mission, which is due to come to an end in 2021, has as its goal: 'Understand origin and evolution of Jupiter, look for solid planetary core, map magnetic field, measure water and ammonia in deep atmosphere, and observe auroras.'

What's Planned Next?

The European Space Agency plans to launch its JUpiter ICy moons Explorer (*JUICE*) mission to Jupiter in June 2022. *JUICE* will rely on gravity assists from Venus and Earth to make the 7.6-year cruise to the giant planet. NASA are also planning to launch another mission, *Europa Clipper*, in 2022, which will arrive at Europa by the end of the decade. Both missions will be looking at Europa's water plumes and atmosphere in great detail.

On a more aspirational level, back in 2003, NASA proposed a programme called *HOPE* (Human Outer Planets Exploration). One of its main target destinations was Callisto, one of Jupiter's moons. Scientists know it has a watery ocean beneath its surface, but most importantly, it has a relatively low cosmic radiation loading, meaning that humans could tolerate being there for a few months at a time. Europa experiences a much higher radiation dose, meaning that humans could only remain there for a few days. However, it would take at least 2-3 years to get there - could you cope with being in a spaceship that long?

SATURN

The spectacular rings
of Saturn.

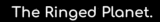
The Ringed Planet.

How Big?
Equatorial Diameters

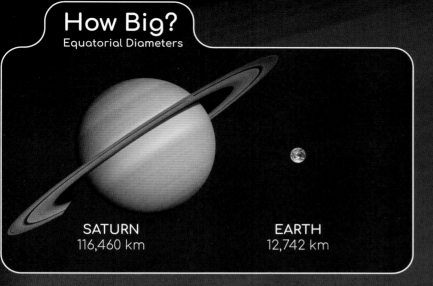

SATURN
116,460 km

EARTH
12,742 km

Atmosphere

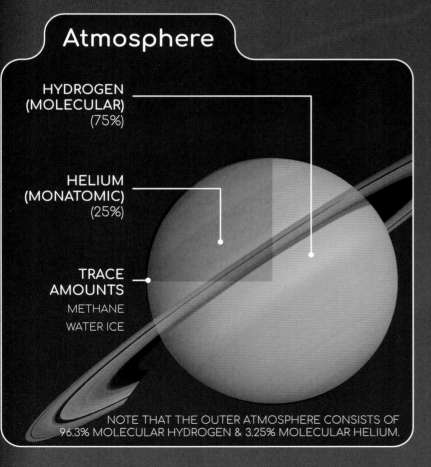

HYDROGEN
(MOLECULAR)
(75%)

HELIUM
(MONATOMIC)
(25%)

TRACE
AMOUNTS
METHANE
WATER ICE

NOTE THAT THE OUTER ATMOSPHERE CONSISTS OF
96.3% MOLECULAR HYDROGEN & 3.25% MOLECULAR HELIUM.

Key Facts

First recorded by humanity:	**'since ancient times'**
First recorded by:	**Rings by Huygens (1659)**
Planet type:	**Gas giant**
Distance from the Sun:	**1.43 billion km**
Mass:	**568.3×10^{24} kg**
Equatorial diameter:	**116,460 km**
Surface area:	**42.7×10^9 km^2**
Surface temperature range:	**-185 °C to -122 °C**
Gravity % compared to Earth:	**106% (10.44 m/s^2)**
Surface atmospheric pressure:	**>1,000 bar**
Main atmosphere gases:	**H_2 (75%); He (25%)**
Number of moons:	**at least 82**
Notable moons:	**Titan; Iapetus; Rhea**
Number of rings:	**Seven main rings**
Strength of magnetic field:	**Weaker than Earth's**
Direction of rotation:	**West to East (26.7° tilt)**
Rotational period (day length):	**10 hrs 42 mins**
Orbital revolution (year length):	**10,585 Earth days**

The Ringed Planet

Saturn is the sixth planet out from the Sun and the second-largest planet in our Solar System. It is known as a gas giant (as is Jupiter) and consists of a massive sphere made mostly of hydrogen (H_2) and a little helium (He). It does not have a solid surface (like Earth or Mars), although it might have a molten, rocky solid core about the size of Earth. However, this has still to be confirmed. It is characterised by the colossal rings of interplanetary icebergs that surround the planet.

Saturn is 1.4748 billion km (~886 million miles) from the Sun. Like all planets, the distance between Saturn and the Earth varies depending upon the position of each in their respective orbits. Saturn orbits around the Sun once every 29.4 Earth years.

The planet travels at an average speed of 34,821 kilometers per hour (21,637 miles per hour) in its orbit around the Sun, which makes it the slowest orbiting planet.

Saturn is a huge planet: nine Earths packed side-by-side would fit into the planet's diameter, and that doesn't include its rings. The planet itself (excluding its rings) has a radius of 60,300 km. It is one of the five planets that can be seen in our night sky without using a telescope or binoculars.

The planet has been known since ancient times and has been observed for thousands of years by people of many different cultures.

Saturn's Rings

The rings of Saturn form the most extensive ring system of any planet in our Solar System. Saturn isn't the only planet to have rings, but it definitely has the most beautiful and conspicuous ones. The rings consist of countless lumps of water-ice, from 1 cm to 10 m across, that orbit Saturn.

Gravitational forces and angular momentum ensure these lumps maintain their constant distance from Saturn. The rings are aligned to form a thin disc around the planet, the thickness of each ring is between 10 m and 1 km. The densest of the rings extend between 7,000 km and 80,000 km away from Saturn's equator.

Saturn backlit by the Sun. Various rings are visible from this angle.

Saturn's intricate rings.

The rings of Saturn form the most extensive ring system of any planet in our Solar System.

Whilst Saturn itself is about 4.5 billion years old, its rings are thought to be much younger, at between 10 to 100 million years old. Since the rings are constantly losing material, it has been proposed they may disappear completely in another 300 million years.

There are two theories as to how the rings were formed. One is that the rings were once a moon of Saturn whose orbit got gradually closer to the planet until it got ripped apart. A modification of this theory is that the moon disintegrated after being struck by a large comet or asteroid. The second theory is that the rings were never part of a moon, but are instead left over from the original nebular material from which Saturn formed.

Working out from the planet, the main rings are named C, B, and A. This rather bizarre naming system is because they've been named in the order each was discovered. A and B were discovered in 1675 by Giovanni Cassini, C in 1850 and D in 1933. The latest to be discovered was G in 1980 from data sent back by *Voyager 1*. Although seven 'main' rings have been allocated letters, there are in fact many more finer rings in existence around Saturn.

The curious hexagonal cloud pattern at Saturn's North pole.

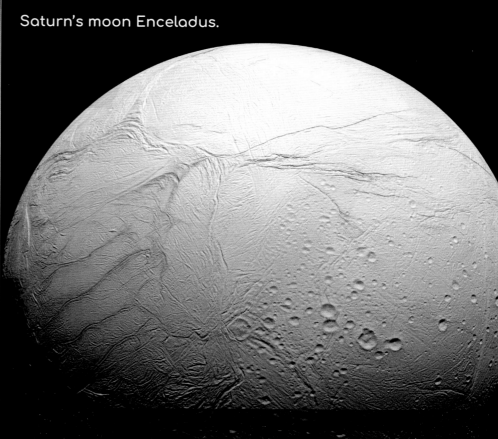

Saturn's moon Enceladus.

Saturn's Moons

Saturn has a total of 82 moons - fifty-three of these are 'known' (meaning they have been given names and descriptions) and 29 are awaiting such recognition.

Saturn's largest moon, Titan, is bigger than our own moon and even bigger than the planet Mercury. It's the second largest moon in the Solar System (the largest being Ganymede, orbiting Jupiter).

It has a predominantly rocky core with an icy surface. It has a very thick atmosphere which mostly consists of nitrogen (similar to Earth's, but with negligible oxygen). The same side of Titan always faces Saturn, so Titan takes 16 days to orbit Saturn and to rotate once.

Saturn also has other icy moons, such as Mimas which has a large crater that is a quarter of the diameter of the whole moon; and Enceladus, which has very dark material covering one side and very bright material covering the other side, but which also possesses a sub-surface ocean of water.

Some of Saturn's smaller moons help keep Saturn's rings stable by orbiting in or near the rings. These moons are called 'shepherd moons' and use their gravity to keep the small ring particles in a stable orbit. Some of the gaps in Saturn's rings are caused by these moons.

Phoebi is one of Saturn's outermost moons.

Phoebe is one of the outermost moons of Saturn, orbiting the planet in a retrograde direction (that is, opposite to Saturn's rotation), at an average distance from the planet of 215 Saturn radii. It was discovered in 1899.

As it was targeted by the Cassini spacecraft in 2004, much is known of this. Phoebe is roughly spherical with a diameter of 213 km (approximately 1/16th that of our Moon). The surface is pockmarked with craters from collisions. It's believed there could be water-ice under its outer surface.

Missions to Saturn

Four spacecraft have flown by Saturn so far. All of these missions have made important discoveries and sent back wonderful close-up images of Saturn, its moons, and its ring system. At its closest, Saturn is 1.2 billion km away from Earth. So with today's spacecraft technology, it takes about eight years for a spacecraft to reach Saturn.

In September 1979, *Pioneer 11* became the first probe to fly by and study Saturn up close (albeit at a distance of 20,900 km away!). *Pioneer 11* was responsible for the discovery of Saturn's F ring. The craft then went on to inspect the environment around Jupiter before achieving escape velocity and departing our Solar System.

Launched in 1977, *Voyager 1* flew by Saturn in November 1980 (at a distance of 64,200 km) and its sister craft *Voyager 2* in August 1981 (at a distance of 41,000 km). These spacecraft studied many of the moons of Saturn as well as some of its rings. *Voyager 1* revealed the existence of the G ring.

In August 2012, *Voyager 1* headed out to interstellar space, followed by its sister in November 2018. Both craft continue to send data back to Earth, even though *Voyager 1* is more than 20 billion km away!

Launched in October 1997, the *Cassini* spacecraft reached Saturn in July 2004. For 13 years it continued to send back observations of the planet, its moons, and its rings. Within this time, it orbited Saturn 294 times. It also carried a probe with it named *Huygens*, which parachuted to the surface of Titan in January 2005.

Huygens returned spectacular images and other science results during a 2.5 hour descent through Titan's hazy atmosphere, before coming to rest amid rounded cobbles of ice on a floodplain damp with liquid methane.

When *Cassini*'s fuel was exhausted, the spacecraft was intentionally directed into Saturn's atmosphere and vapourised on 15th September 2017.

NASA has no plans at the moment to visit Saturn again, although the *Dragonfly* mission, developed and operated by the Johns Hopkins Applied Physics Laboratory, will launch in June 2027.

Astrobiology

Saturn cannot support life as we know it, but Titan and Enceladus might offer suitable conditions.

Titan, Saturn's largest moon, is the only moon in our Solar System that has clouds and a dense atmosphere. Titan has rain, rivers, lakes and seas of liquid methane and ethane. The largest seas are hundreds of metres deep and hundreds of kilometres wide. Water does exist on Titan, but it's bound-up as a thick crust of ice, beneath which, is a global ocean.

Enceladus, the sixth-largest moon of Saturn, is covered with a shell of ice, under which there is a global ocean of liquid water. The *Cassini* space craft discovered geyser-like jets of water vapour, methane and other volatiles which could be signatures of life. The discovery of escaping internal heat shows that Enceladus is geologically active, perhaps with hydrothermal vents on the ocean floor.

The sub-surface oceans of Titan and Enceladus might harbour sub-surface vents of super-heated water similar to the 'black smokers' on Earth's seabeds. These might support communities of organisms that exist via chemosynthesis (similar to those found on Earth, see page 75).

Titan, one of Saturn's most mysterious moons.

The surface of Titan by the Huygens probe.

An artist's impression of Enceladus' global sub-surface ocean.

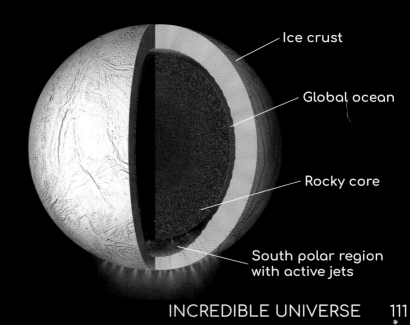

Ice crust

Global ocean

Rocky core

South polar region with active jets

URANUS

Uranus is the seventh planet from the Sun.

How Big?
Equatorial Diameters

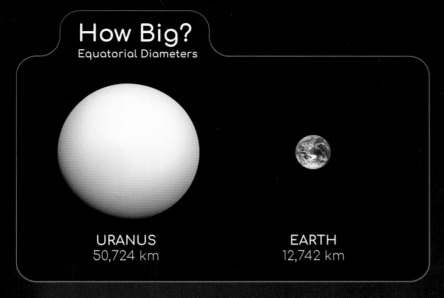

URANUS
50,724 km

EARTH
12,742 km

Atmosphere

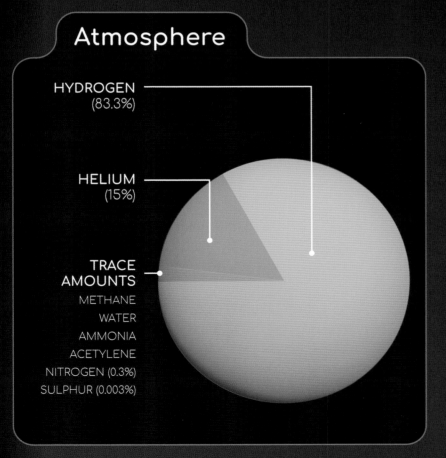

HYDROGEN
(83.3%)

HELIUM
(15%)

TRACE
AMOUNTS

METHANE
WATER
AMMONIA
ACETYLENE
NITROGEN (0.3%)
SULPHUR (0.003%)

Key Facts

First recorded by humanity:	**1781**
First recorded by:	**William Herschel (UK)**
Planet type:	**Ice-gas giant**
Distance from the Sun:	**2.87 billion km**
Mass:	**86.81x10²⁴kg**
Equatorial diameter:	**50,724 km**
Surface area:	**8.083 x 10⁹ km²**
Surface temperature range:	**-224.2 °C to -170.2 °C**
Gravity % compared to Earth:	**89% (8.69 m/s²)**
Surface atmospheric pressure:	**>1,000 bar**
Main atmosphere gases:	**H₂, He + Methane (CH₄)**
Number of moons:	**at least 27**
Notable moons:	**Titania and Oberon**
Number of rings:	**13 known faint rings**
Strength of magnetic field:	**Moderate but offset**
Direction of rotation:	**East to West (98° tilt)**
Rotational period (day length):	**17 hrs 14 mins**
Orbital revolution (year length):	**(84 Earth years)**

An Ice Giant

Uranus is the seventh planet from the Sun. It has the third largest planetary radius and the fourth largest mass. The planet is named after the Greek god of the sky, who was father to Cronus (Saturn) and grandfather to Zeus (Jupiter). Along with Neptune, Uranus is classified as an 'ice giant', distinguishing it from the 'gas giants' of Jupiter and Saturn.

Although Uranus may appear uniform when viewed in visible light, immense storms do rage through it atmosphere (but are generally less visible than the storms on other giant planets). Uranus has the coldest atmosphere in the Solar System, with a minimum temperature of -224 °C.

Uranus is the only planet within the Solar System which rotates on its side. Its axis of rotation is actually almost in the same plane as its solar orbit. Put another way, instead of spinning it's rolling. Its north and south poles lie where most other planets have their equators. It's thought this has come about following a collision it had with another Earth-sized 'protoplanet', sometime during the formation of the Solar System. It also spins in the opposite direction than most of the other planets (except for Venus), that is, from east to west.

Uranus was discovered by William Herschel, the German-born British astronomer, in 1781. Previous to his sightings, the faint celestial body had been recorded as a star. However, when viewed through his homemade reflecting telescope, Herschel determined it must be a comet. He was later convinced by colleagues that it was indeed a new planet. In recognition of his achievement, the king (George III), gave Herschel an annual stipend of £200 (equivalent to £25,000 in today's money) on condition that he move to Windsor, so the Royal Family could look through his telescopes!

Characteristics

Uranus's mass is approximately 14.5 times that of the Earth, making it the least massive of the giant planets. Its internal structure consists of a rocky (silicate/iron-nickel) core, a large mantle (extending for about 60% of the radius) and an outer gaseous hydrogen-helium envelope. The mantle is described by scientists as 'icy', but it is actually a hot and dense fluid consisting of water, ammonia and other volatiles.

Uranus maintains a surprisingly low internal temperature, with very little heat escaping from the planet. Quite why this is so is not known. The extreme pressure deep within Uranus may cause carbon atoms to condense into crystals of diamonds which rain down through the mantle like hailstones (as is also thought to happen on the three other giant planets).

Uranus does not have a definite, solid surface, yet the outermost part of its gaseous envelope is referred to as an atmosphere. This consists of molecular hydrogen (H_2), helium (He) and a small amount of methane (CH_4). This methane fraction absorbs red wavelengths of visible light, resulting in the planet taking on an aquamarine or cyan colour.

Uranus produces a magnetic field but, as with some of its other oddities, it is peculiar in that it is asymmetrical. Neptune also has a similar displaced and tilted magnetic field, so scientists think this may be a characteristic of ice giants. It may be that the field is not being generated from the planet's core but from its mantle.

Thirteen distinct rings have been identified around Uranus, composed of extremely dark, small particles ranging in size from millimetres to tens of centimetres. It is likely the rings are much younger than the planet, possibly resulting from the shattering of a moon following a powerful impact. Two of the rings lie well away from Uranus and were only detected by the Hubble Telescope in 2005.

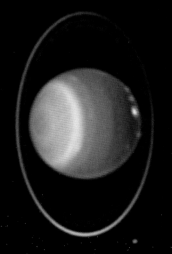

A false-colour image of Uranus showing cloud bands, rings, and moons obtained by the Hubble Space Telescope's NICMOS camera.

Uranus's rings, the southern collar and a bright cloud in the northern hemisphere.

Features

As a result of its peculiar axial tilt, each pole of Uranus experiences 42 years of continuous sunlight followed by 42 years of complete darkness. Averaged over a Uranian year (84 Earth years), the polar regions of Uranus receive a greater energy input from the Sun than its equatorial regions. Even so, Uranus is hotter at its equator than at its poles! Quite why this should be so has yet to be discovered.

Uranus's atmosphere is bland in comparison to the other giant planets, even to Neptune, which it otherwise closely resembles. When *Voyager 2* flew by in 1986, just 10 cloud features were noted across the whole planet. However, since then, other studies have shown there to be larger and more numerous cloud formations from time to time. Winds also occur, being most noticeable at the equator. Here they are retrograde in motion, meaning they travel against the direction of spin, whereas closer to the poles they are prograde, moving in the same direction as the spin.

Moons

Uranus has 27 known moons or natural satellites. These have all been named after characters from the works of Shakespeare and Alexander Pope. The five main moons are Miranda, Ariel, Unbriel, Titania and Oberon. They are all conglomerates

Uranus is one of the least-visited planets of the Solar System.

of ice and rock, the ice including ammonia and carbon dioxide. Titania is the largest, being about half the size of our own Moon. Back in 1986, the scientists controlling the *Voyager 2* space probe were amazed at what they saw when Miranda came into view. It looked nothing like any of the other moons in the Solar System. It looked as though it had been ripped to pieces and then shoved back together again. Enormous gashes were apparent, some with cliffs over 10 km tall!

Missions to Uranus

There has only been one mission which has targeted Uranus and that was NASA's *Voyager 2*. This probe was launched on 20th August 1977 and had its closest encounter with Uranus on 24th January 1986, coming to within 81,500 km of its cloud tops. Having taken 9.5 years to get there, it had just six hours to find out as much as it could, before its trajectory took it off to Neptune.

Uranus' icy moon Miranda.

Almost all of our detailed knowledge about Uranus has come from this mission. *Voyager 2* sent back data on the structure and chemical composition of the planet's atmosphere and also on its magnetic field. It went on to investigate five of its largest moons and the composition of its rings before heading on its way to Neptune.

A number of follow-up missions to Uranus have been proposed by NASA, but none, so far, has been approved.

Astrobiology

Uranus's environment is not conducive to life as we know it. The temperatures, pressures, and materials that characterise this planet are most likely too extreme and volatile for organisms to adapt to.

NEPTUNE

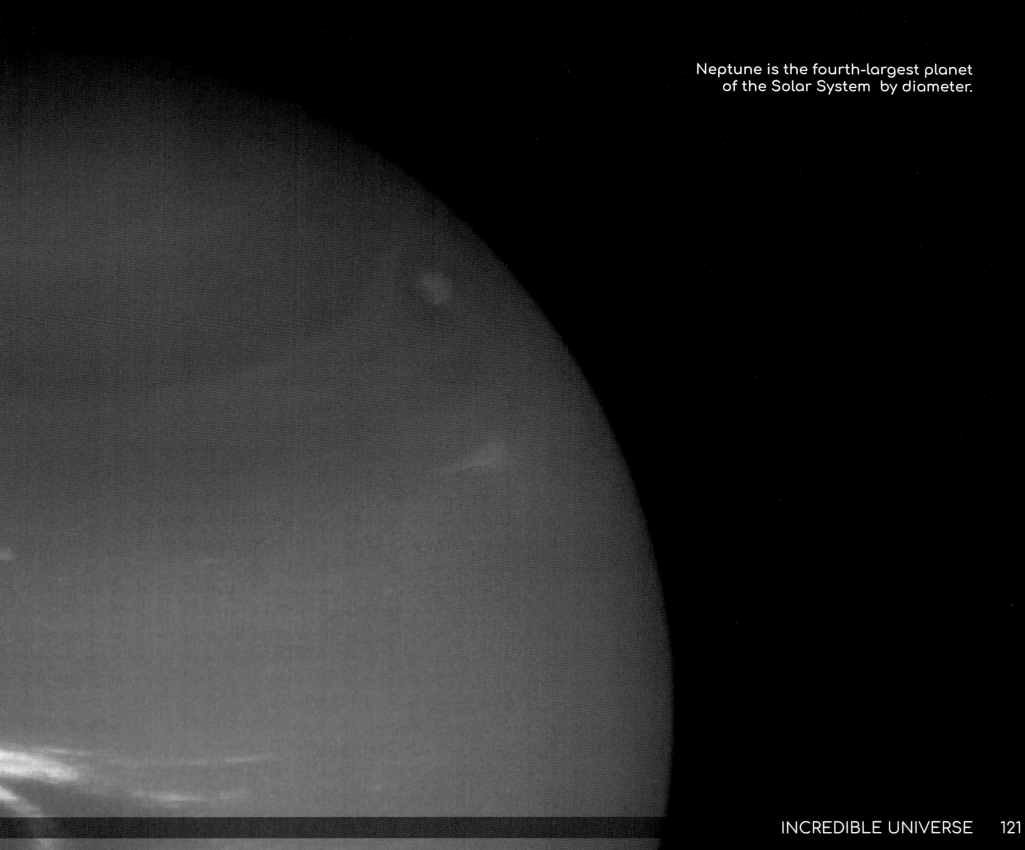

Neptune is the fourth-largest planet
of the Solar System by diameter.

Neptune - the blue planet.

How Big?
Equatorial Diameters

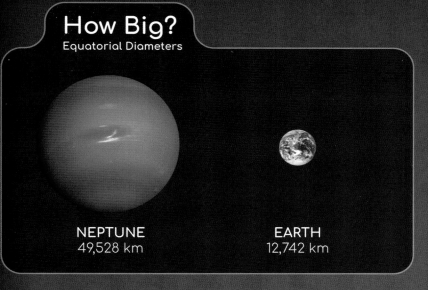

NEPTUNE
49,528 km

EARTH
12,742 km

Atmosphere

HYDROGEN
(MOLECULAR)
(~80%)

HELIUM
(~19%)

METHANE
(~1.5%)

TRACE
AMOUNTS

AMMONIA ICE

WATER ICE

AMMONIA
HYDROSULPHIDE

Key Facts

First recorded by humanity: **1846**

First recorded by: **Galle & Le Verrier**

Planet type: **Ice giant**

Distance from the Sun: **4.49 billion km**

Mass: **102.4×10^{24} kg**

Equatorial diameter: **49,528 km**

Surface area: **7.618×10^{9} km^2**

Surface temperature range: **-201 °C (mean)**

Gravity % compared to Earth: **114% (11.15 m/s^2)**

Surface atmospheric pressure: **>1,000 bar**

Main atmosphere gases: **H$_2$ (80%); He (19%); CH$_4$ (1%)**

Number of moons: **at least 14**

Notable moons: **Triton; Hippocamp**

Number of rings: **Six narrow rings known**

Strength of magnetic field: **Very strong, offset**

Direction of rotation: **West to East (28.3° tilt)**

Rotational period (day length): **16 hrs 6 mins**

Orbital revolution (year length): **(164.8 Earth years)**

The Blue Planet

Neptune is named after the Roman god of the sea. It is the eighth and most remote planet of the Solar System, being 4.5 billion km from the Sun and 4.3 billion km from Earth. Within the Solar System, it is the fourth largest planet by diameter, the third most massive planet, and the densest giant planet. It is 57 times the volume of the Earth, though 17 time its mass.

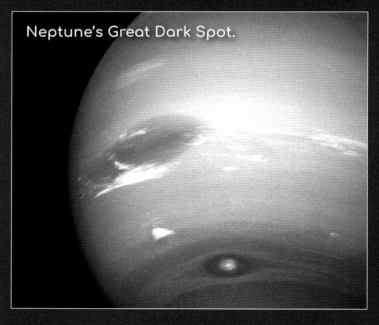

Neptune's Great Dark Spot.

Most unusually, Neptune was predicted to exist before it was actually observed. Although Galileo Galilei in 1613 marked the position of Neptune on his astronomical chart, it's believed he thought it a star, appearing close to Jupiter in the night sky. It wasn't until the 1830s that a French astronomer, Alexis Bouvard, who was studying the orbit of Uranus, noted that the orbit had an irregularity which he surmised was the result of the gravitational pull of another astronomical body which he was unable to detect with his telescope. After his death in 1843, the position of this body was calculated by Urbain Le Verrier (another French astronomer and mathematician), and the new planet was then discovered in 1846 by a colleague of Le Verrier, the German astronomer Johann Galle. Le Verrier wanted to name 'his' new planet after himself, but his fellow astronomers thought it should bear a mythological name like the other planets, so the name Neptune was agreed.

Neptune was visited by NASA's *Voyager 2* space probe when it made a flyby on 25th August 1989 (having been launched in 1977). It is the only spacecraft to have visited the planet. The Hubble telescope (launched in 1990) and large, ground-based telescopes have since provided more details of Neptune's physical and chemical attributes.

Neptune is known as an 'ice giant', together with Uranus. This distinguishes the two of them from the 'gas giants' of Jupiter and Saturn. Neptune has a liquid core of iron, nickel and silicates, whose temperature is over 5,000 °C. The mantle consists of water, ammonia and methane in a fluid state. Closer to the core, it is thought that the methane molecules (CH_4) lose their hydrogen atoms and form diamonds (pure carbon) which rain downwards like hailstones!

Neptune's rings.

Bands of high-altitude clouds cast shadows on Neptune's lower cloud deck.

Neptune's Rings

The first of Neptune's rings was discovered in 1968 and subsequently several more have been observed. They are far less prominent than those around Saturn and also far less stable. Some have been found to be arcs, or partial circles, which had been unexpected and has been explained by the gravitational force created by the moon Galatea.

It is thought the rings comprise ice particles coated with silicates or carbon-based material. The photo here, taken on a 10 minute exposure, shows several rings, some very bright and distinct with others much fainter and broader.

Clouds and Storms

Neptune's outer atmosphere consists of 80% hydrogen (H_2), 19% helium (He) and trace amounts of methane (CH_4). Methane is known to absorb red wavelengths of light, resulting in the planet appearing a blue colour, though a darker blue than Uranus. Lower down in the atmosphere are clouds of hydrogen sulphide (H_2S), ammonia (NH_3) and water (H_2O).

Neptune also experiences weather variations, with incredible wind speeds of 2,200 km/h (1,300 mph) being generated. Most of the winds move in the opposite direction to the rotation of the planet. A large feature known as the 'Great Dark Spot', close to the equator, marked a vast area where storms continually rage, although this spot now appears to have disappeared! Instead, new dark spots have appeared, again probably signifying areas of great storms.

Neptune's Moons

Neptune has 14 moons, the largest of which is Triton, discovered just 17 days after the discovery of Neptune in 1846. The other moons have taken far longer to find, with a second, Nereid, being discovered in 1949 and a third, Larissa, in 1981. It was not until *Voyager 2*'s flyby in 1989 that most of the others were identified. The 14th moon, Hippocamp (meaning half-horse and half-fish), was found as recently as 2013 after careful, detailed study of images from the Hubble space telescope.

Proteus is Neptune's second largest moon. As a result of its dark surface and the fact that it orbits very close to Neptune, it remained undiscovered until 1989. Unlike most moons, Proteus is not spherical. Instead it has a box-like shape. If its mass was a little larger, its own gravity would cause it to reform into a sphere.

Of all of Neptune's moons, Triton is the most interesting. It is known as an 'irregular' moon, meaning that its orbit is retrograde (that is, in the opposite direction to Neptune's rotation). This, together with its composition being very similar to Pluto's, has led astronomers to think Triton was originally a dwarf planet captured from the Kuiper belt. It also has a circular (rather than elliptical) orbit.

Triton is one of the coldest bodies in the Solar System, with a thick outer crust of water-ice. The surface temperature has been measured at -235 °C! The tenuous atmosphere close to the surface is composed of nitrogen, methane, carbon dioxide and water, whilst higher up it's mostly nitrogen with small amounts of methane and carbon monoxide.

Triton.

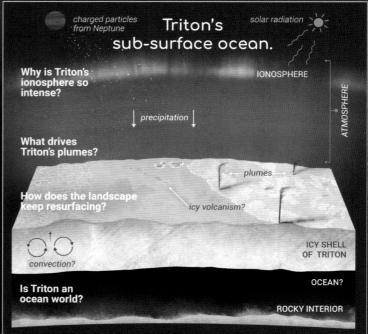

Triton's sub-surface ocean.

charged particles from Neptune

solar radiation

Why is Triton's ionosphere so intense?

IONOSPHERE

ATMOSPHERE

precipitation

What drives Triton's plumes?

plumes

How does the landscape keep resurfacing?

icy volcanism?

ICY SHELL OF TRITON

convection?

OCEAN?

Is Triton an ocean world?

ROCKY INTERIOR

Another area of interest is Triton's ionosphere, a region of charged particles around the whole moon, similar to what exists around Earth. However, the Triton ionosphere is ten times more intense than around any other moon in the Solar System. Usually ionospheres around icy bodies are driven by the Sun, so how is it there's one around Triton? This remains a mystery.

On its flyby, *Voyager 2* recorded geysers spouting dark material to a height of 8 km out of the polar cap on Triton. It's not known what causes such eruptions. However, there are strong indications that there is liquid water deep inside Triton, forming a subterranean ocean.

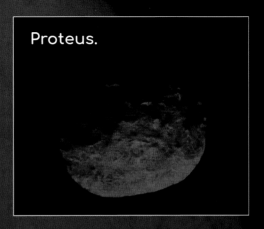
Proteus.

As a result of its retrograde orbit and relative proximity to Neptune (closer than our Moon is to Earth), tidal deceleration is causing Triton to spiral inward, which will lead to its eventual destruction. However, this won't happen within your lifetime - it's estimated it will take another 3.6 billion years!

Future Missions to Neptune

As only one spacecraft has ever approached Neptune, there's considerable interest in sending more missions to investigate this cold blue planet further. The China National Space Administration is considering launching a pair of *Voyager*-like probes, named Interstellar Express, in 2024. One of the probes would fly-by Neptune in January 2038, passing only 1,000 km above its cloud tops.

NASA is considering a proposed mission entitled *Neptune Odyssey*. The craft would incorporate an orbiter and an atmospheric probe. It would be launched sometime between 2031 and 2033, reaching Neptune in 2049. Another possible NASA mission is simply named Triton. This is still in a 'study phase', meaning that it has not yet been selected to go ahead. The plan is for it to find out more about Triton's subterranean ocean, its polar plumes and its ionosphere.

Astrobiology

Neptune could not harbour life as we know it, but the prospect of geothermal vent communities of organisms in the sub-surface oceans of Triton is a possibility, similar to Saturn's moons (see page 111).

THE KUIPER BELT AND DWARF PLANETS

The Northern hemisphere of Pluto.

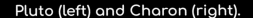

Pluto (left) and Charon (right).

The Kuiper belt is a ring of objects in the outer Solar System, extending from the orbit of Neptune at 30 astronomical units to approximately 50 astronomical units from the Sun.

It is similar to the Asteroid Belt, but is far larger – 20 times as wide and 20–200 times as massive.

Like the Asteroid Belt, it consists mainly of small bodies or remnants from when the Solar System formed. While many asteroids are composed primarily of rock and metal, most Kuiper belt objects are composed largely of frozen volatiles (termed 'ices'), such as methane, ammonia and water.

The Kuiper belt is home to three objects identified as dwarf planets: Pluto (approximately 2,360 km in diameter), Haumea (approximately 1,540 km in diameter) and Makemake (approximately 1,430 km in diameter). Some of the Solar System's moons, such as Neptune's Triton and Saturn's Phoebe, may have originated in the Kuiper belt.

PLUTO

The dwarf planet Pluto.

How Big?
Equatorial Diameters

PLUTO
2,377 km

EARTH
12,742 km

Atmosphere

NITROGEN
(MOLECULAR)
(~99%)

METHANE
(~0.25%)

TRACE GASES

CARBON
MONOXIDE
(~0.07%)

OTHER TRACE
ELEMENTS AND
COMPOUNDS

Key Facts

First recorded by humanity: **1930**

First recorded by: **Clyde Tombaugh (USA)**

Planet type: **Dwarf Planet**

Distance from the Sun: **6 billion km**

Mass: **1.30900 x 10^{22} kg**

Equatorial diameter: **2,376.6 km**

Surface area: **16.7 x 106 km²**

Surface temperature range: **-240 °C to -218 °C**

Gravity % compared to Earth: **6.3% (0.620 m/s²)**

Surface atmospheric pressure: **<0.1 bar**

Main atmosphere gases: **N_2, CH_4, CO**

Number of moons: **at least 5**

Notable moons: **Charon; Hydra; Nix**

Number of rings: **None**

Strength of magnetic field: **Not known**

Direction of rotation: **East to West (57° tilt)**

Rotational period (day length): **6.39 Earth days**

Orbital revolution (year length): **248 Earth years**

Pluto is classified as a dwarf planet. It is relatively small (one-third of the volume of our Moon) yet remains the ninth largest object orbiting the Sun. Its orbit around the Sun is 'moderately eccentric', meaning that its distance from the Sun can vary between 4.5 billion km and 7.35 billion km. This means that Pluto, periodically, comes closer to the Sun than Neptune does. Light from the Sun takes 5.5 hours to reach Pluto (by comparison, it takes 8 mins. and 20 secs. for sunlight to reach Earth).

Pluto was discovered in 1930, lying beyond Neptune in the outlying regions of our Solar System, and was originally identified as the ninth planet orbiting our Sun.

At the start of the 1990s, its designation as a planet was questioned. At the time, several other similar-sized bodies were being discovered within the Kuiper belt, a collection of remnants from when the Solar System formed, which forms a vast, disparate ring, between about 4.5-7.5 billion km from the Sun. So it was reclassified from being a planet to being a dwarf planet.

Pluto is the only world (so far) named by an 11-year-old girl and not by an astronomer. In 1930, Venetia Burney of Oxford, England, suggested to her grandfather that the new discovery be named after the Roman god of the underworld. He forwarded the name to the Lowell Observatory in the USA (where its discovery had been made) and it was selected.

Since July 2015, when NASA's *New Horizons* spacecraft made a flyby, our knowledge of Pluto has grown considerably.

Internal Structure and Atmosphere

Pluto is about two-thirds the diameter of Earth's Moon and probably has a rocky core surrounded by a mantle of water ice. Interesting ices like methane and nitrogen coat the surface with a frost-like covering. Due to its lower density, Pluto's mass is about one-sixth that of Earth's Moon.

Pluto has a thin, tenuous atmosphere that expands when the orbit of the dwarf planet comes closer to the Sun and collapses as it moves farther away. The main constituent of its atmosphere is molecular nitrogen (N_2), though molecules of methane (CH_4) and carbon monoxide (CO) have also been detected. When Pluto is close to the Sun, its surface ices sublimate (changing directly from solids to gases) and rise to temporarily form a thin atmosphere. Pluto's low gravity (about 6% of Earth's) causes the atmosphere to be much more extended in altitude than our planet's atmosphere.

When Pluto is travelling away from the Sun, surface temperatures drop and it becomes much colder. During this time, the bulk of the planet's atmosphere may freeze and fall as snow to the surface. It isn't known whether Pluto has a magnetic field, but its small size and slow rotation suggest it has little or none.

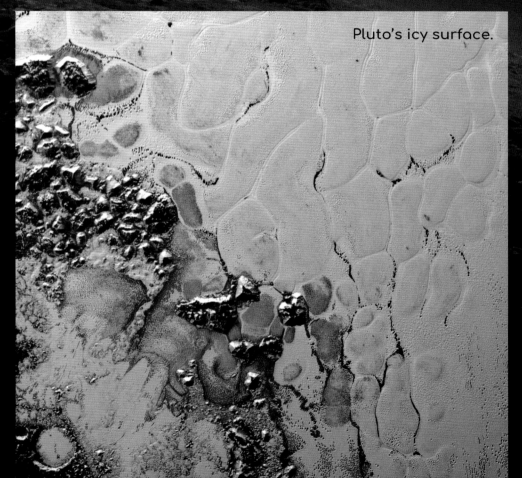

Pluto's icy surface.

Surface Features

Pluto is a complex and mysterious world with mountains, valleys, plains, craters, and maybe glaciers. The tallest mountains are 2 to 3 km high.

They are formed of big blocks of water ice, sometimes with a coating of frozen gases like methane. Long troughs and valleys, some as long as 600 kilometers, add to this strange world's interesting features.

Craters as large as 260 kilometers in diameter dot some of the landscape on Pluto, with some showing signs of erosion and filling. This suggests tectonic forces are slowly resurfacing Pluto.

The most prominent plains observed on Pluto appear to be made of frozen nitrogen gas and show no craters.

Moons

Pluto has five known moons: Charon, Nix, Hydra, Kerberos, and Styx. These names also refer to characters associated by the ancient Greeks with the underworld.

It is thought that all of these moons might have formed by a collision between Pluto and another similar-sized body early in the history of the Solar System.

Charon (background image) is the biggest of Pluto's moons. It's about half the size of Pluto itself, making it the largest satellite relative to the planet it orbits in our Solar System.

It orbits Pluto at a distance of 19,640 km. For comparison, our Moon is 20 times further away from Earth (at 384,400 km). As they're so close, Pluto and Charon are sometimes referred to as a 'double planet' (see page 129).

Charon's orbit around Pluto takes 153 hours – the same time it takes Pluto to complete one rotation.

This means Charon neither rises nor sets, but hovers over the same spot on Pluto's surface.

The same side of Charon always faces Pluto, a state called 'tidal locking'.

Pluto's other four moons are much smaller, less than 160 kilometers wide. They're also irregularly shaped, not spherical like Charon. Unlike many other moons in the Solar System, these moons are not tidally locked to Pluto. They all spin and don't keep the same face towards Pluto.

Charon.

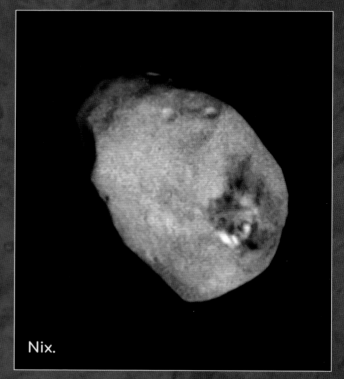

Nix.

Missions to Pluto

To date, there has only been one mission to Pluto and that was NASA's *New Horizons* probe which was launched on 19th January 2006.

Following a brief encounter with an asteroid in June 2006, and a flyby of Jupiter in February 2007 (which provided a 'gravity assist' or slingshot to speed it up), its next destination was Pluto which it approached in early 2015.

Weirdly, when *New Horizons* was launched, Pluto was still a planet, but by the time it got to its destination, Pluto had been reclassified as a dwarf planet!

Its mission at Pluto was to understand how Pluto and its moons had formed; map its surface and that of its moon Charon; assess the atmospheres of both bodies; and search for rings around Pluto (none was found). Scientists were delighted with how well this part of the mission went.

It took a full 15 months for all the data the craft had obtained in a day (6.25 GB) to be sent back to Earth (at a speed of 1-2 kB/s).

Once the fly-by was completed, *New Horizons* headed off towards the Kuiper Belt, where it is hoped it will be able to 'interact' with some of the material which makes up this vast region of the outer Solar System. On 17 April 2021, New Horizons had reached a distance of 50 Astronomical Units (7.5 billion km) from the Sun, and remained fully operational.

At the moment, there are no further missions being planned to revisit Pluto.

Astrobiology

The surface of Pluto is extremely cold (its average temperature is -232°C), so it seems unlikely that life could exist there. Pluto's interior is warmer, and some think there could even be an ocean deep inside which might open the possibility of life supported by geothermal activity. Further observations are required.

EXPLORING MARS

The planet Mars has fascinated star-gazers and astronomers for millennia. The earliest records were made by ancient Egyptians in the 2nd millennium BCE. Since then there have been studies undertaken by the ancient civilisations of China, Mesopotamia, Greece and India. The planet's blood red colour is thought to be the reason why the Romans named it Mars after their god of war.

It took until the 16th century for a heliocentric model of the Solar System to be proposed by Nicolaus Copernicus, where the planets revolve around the Sun. This was later revised by Johannes Kepler who proposed an elliptical orbit for Mars, thus producing a much better fit for various measured observations.

The first telescopic observations of the planet were by Galileo Galilei in 1610, and by the 1670s the first maps were being made of its features, including the polar ice caps. As the quality and magnification of telescopes improved, do did the details of what was being seen.

The dusty landscape of the Red Planet.

By the late 19th century, the Italian Giovanni Schiaparelli described a network of *canali* in the equatorial regions of the planet. This term was translated into English as 'canals', but more accurately should have been 'channels'.

By the turn of the century there was even speculation that they were engineered irrigation canals, constructed by a civilisation of intelligent aliens indigenous to Mars.

An American astronomer, Percival Lowell, was so convinced of the canal theory he even wrote three books on the subject between 1895 and 1908.

It took the British naturalist Alfred Russell Wallace in 1907 to debunk the whole idea in his book *Is Mars habitable?*

With the advent of better optics, the 'canals' were revealed to be an optical illusion, and it was realised that there were no civilisations on the Red Planet. Still, many astrobiologists regard Mars as one of the best candidates for harbouring simple life (see page 85).

NASA's *Curiosity* rover.

What is Mars like?

When viewed from Earth, Mars might appear to be pretty similar to Earth. As we've gradually been able to inspect the planet at closer quarters however, it's become apparent that there are many major differences between the two worlds.

To start with, Mars currently has a very thin atmosphere (though it was denser in the past). Its pressure is just 1% of what we experience on Earth. 96% of it is made up of CO_2, so it would be poisonous for humans to breathe. It also means that any water that may have been present on the surface in the past has evaporated due to its much lower boiling point. However, although no water is present on the surface now, it may well have been in the past. It's thought water may still be present *below* the surface however (see p. 151). Water ice has certainly been detected beneath the surface of the polar regions (*Planum Boreum* [N] and *Planum Australe* [S]).

The rotation period of Mars (its day length or 'sol') has been determined as being 24 hr 37 min 6.22 sec. A Martian year (the time it takes for a complete orbit of the Sun) takes 687 Earth days or 668 sols (Martian days). As a result, Earth makes almost two full orbits in the time it takes Mars to make just one, resulting in the occurrence of Martian oppositions (when the Earth is exactly in between the Sun and Mars) about every 26 months. This is when the Earth is closest to Mars (at about 55 .7 million km) and offers optimal windows for missions to Mars to take place.

The average surface temperature is -63 °C, with a maximum temperature of 35 °C at noon in summer at the equator, and a minimum of about -143 °C in winter at the poles. Even during a Martian day, the temperature can go from 0 °C at midday to -100 °C at night.

Another difference with Earth is the relative gravity. We're used to the pull of gravity being 9.8 m/s^2, but on Mars it's just 3.7 m/s^2. (On our Moon, it's a mere 1.6 m/s^2). It's weaker than Earth's gravity because of Mars's smaller mass.

Mars appears red from Earth because the rocks and soil have a high content of iron oxides, making it appear like rust. The surface of the whole planet is also pock-marked with hundreds of thousands of craters. The largest of these is *Hellas Planitia*, 23,000 km across and 9 km deep! The very thin atmosphere means that almost all meteors hit the surface rather than burning up on entry.

The highest feature on Mars is known as *Olympus Mons*. It's an enormous shield volcano, with a height of over 21.9 km (or 2.5x the height of Mt Everest from sea level). It has a roughly circular footprint which covers an area equivalent to the size of Italy (300,000 km^2). As such, it is one of the largest volcanoes in our Solar System.

Missions to Mars

In recent decades, our knowledge of Mars has expanded dramatically, partly through observations from the Hubble telescope, but primarily because we have managed to send spacecraft to orbit the planet (orbiters) and, most recently, to actually land on its surface (static craft and mobile rovers).

Starting in the early 1960s, 49 missions have been sent to Mars. Of these, there has been a failure rate of roughly half, including those that failed to reach the planet and those than failed to operate successfully once there. Successful missions are hard to come by, as they are so technically complicated - there are so many things that can go wrong!

On 2nd December 1971, the USSR's *Mars-3 lander* was the first spacecraft to land softly on Mars. Whilst it was able to communicate this fact to its jubilant controllers, within two minutes the signal went dead. The reason for this isn't clear. Another catastrophe happened when NASA's *Mars Climate Orbiter*, launched in 1998, was put in the wrong trajectory due to its engineers mixing up metric and imperial units!

All NASA spacecraft launched to Mars since 1999 - from the *Spirit*, *Opportunity* and *Curiosity* rovers, to orbiting craft such as *Mars Odyssey* and *Mars Reconnaissance Orbiter* - have not only succeeded but have operated long past their prime mission durations.

Perseverance Rover

The most recent, most sophisticated and most expensive (costing $2 billion!) rover to have landed on Mars is NASA's *Perseverance* which launched from Florida on 30th July 2020 and safely touched down in Jezero crater on Mars on 18th February 2021. The successful landing of this car-sized rover, together with its companion mini-helicopter called *Ingenuity*, is arguably one of the greatest achievements of humankind.

An artist's impression of NASA's *Perseverance* rover deploying on the surface of Mars.

Olympus Mons.

An artist's impression of Ingenuity.

The landing procedure was complex but was completed perfectly. The landing capsule headed towards the ground at a phenomenal 16,000 km/hr! Mars's thin atmosphere slowed the descent (the heat shield heated to over 1,300 °C). At 10 km above the ground, the heat shield was jettisoned and then a parachute was deployed, at 2 km up, thruster rockets helped slow the craft down further.

At 20 m above the surface, the 'sky crane', still firing its thrusters, then lowered the rover on cables to the surface. Once it was safely down, the cables were cut and the rocket stage shot off, ending up crashing some distance away. All of the commands to execute the landing successfully had been pre-programmed. Mission controllers had to wait an agonising '7 minutes of terror' during the whole landing phase before *Perseverance* radioed to say it had arrived safely (a message which took 11 minutes to reach Earth!).

After checking all of its circuits were working properly, the 6-wheeled *Perseverance* rover slowly rolled off its platform and then lifted out *Ingenuity* from its underbelly. This mini-helicopter was aptly named. Mars's thin atmosphere meant that a double propeller had to be used, each prop turning in opposite directions at very high speed, in order to generate the thrust needed to get it off the ground. Its purpose was to search for interesting rocks which *Perseverance*, with its cameras and drills, could then investigate further.

Perseverance's mission is to search for signs of ancient life and to collect samples of rock and regolith intended for eventual return to Earth by another mission. The acquisition of these samples is another task that has had to be cleverly worked out.

On board *Perseverance* is a multi-use, extendable, robotic arm, a camera called Watson for colour images and a laser camera called Sherloc. The arm has various scientific instruments, including a sophisticated drill. This is used to core out a chunk of rock, which is then carefully stored in a sealed metal canister inside the main body of the rover.

The plan is for these rock sample tubes, once sealed, to be left on the ground and await their collection by another rover to pick them up on a future Mars mission. They will then be transferred to a launch vehicle which, together with the help of a small craft in orbit around Mars, will have the capability to bring the sample tubes all the way back to Earth. In a purpose-built, ultra-clean lab, scientists will be able to analyse their contents. However, we may have to wait until 2031 for this to happen!

Geological Structure of Mars

The covering of loose material that covers underlying rock is called regolith. It can consist of fine dust, sand, pebbles, small rocks and larger boulders. All of these types of rock, from minute sand grains right up to large angular boulders, together with exposed 'solid' rock formations (often referred to as bedrock), all add to the story of what Mars is made of, and what geological processes have happened during its 4.6 billion year history.

The data that have been (and still are being) sent back from both orbiters and rovers are providing Mars scientists with new insights into the planet's geology and features almost on a daily basis.

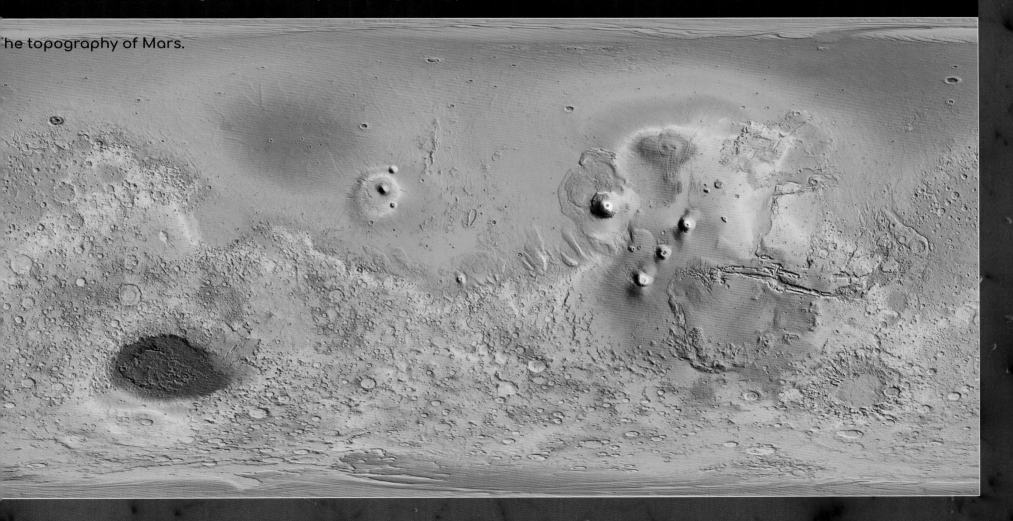

The topography of Mars.

Mars has certainly had its fair share of meteoroid impacts during its lifetime. It has the greatest diversity of impact crater types of any planet in our Solar System.

Over 42,000 craters greater than 5 km in diameter have now been catalogued, although there are many hundreds of thousands more that are smaller than this. On the more recent craters, fresh 'ejector' material can be seen spreading out from the impact sites.

With the exception of the polar regions, almost all surfaces on Mars are covered by a fine dust, which forms the major constituent of the soil on Mars.

From time to time, dust devils (twisters) occur, formed by localised winds, which travel across the plains at speed and produce tall plumes of dust.

The Martian landscape.

Liquid water appears to have been common on the surface of Mars during the past. Flowing water carved the surface, forming networks of valleys and produced sediment. The positive confirmation of the presence of water is very important, as it will give a good indication that primitive life might have existed on the planet in the past.

The landing site for *Perseverance* within Jezero crater was chosen because it was close to what looks like a delta of ancient water channels entering the crater. It's hoped that this is where evidence of primitive life will be found within the sedimentary rocks beneath the surface.

The discovery of rounded gravels (worn smooth by being rolled along by water flows) and sediments is a great start to this investigation.

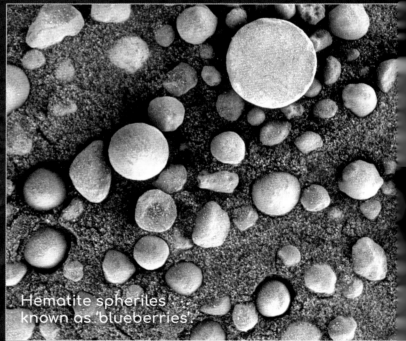

Hematite spheriles known as 'blueberries'.

In 2004, NASA's *Opportunity* rover came across scatterings of small (2-4 mm in diameter), spherical, hard, grey spherules, composed of the mineral hematite (see bottom image on page 144). These were nicknamed 'blueberries', as they appeared blue in false-colour images. Such spherules are known to be formed in the ground by water, so this was another positive indication that water was once present in these areas.

Mars's Early Atmosphere and Climate

Today, the atmosphere on Mars is far thinner than Earth's atmosphere. But it was not always so. Millions of years ago, Mars's atmosphere was much denser, providing greater pressure and much warmer conditions at ground level. These conditions enabled liquid water to exist on the surface of the planet, possibly as vast oceans.

But over hundreds of millions of years, much of the Martian atmosphere has been lost to space. Several processes caused the loss of Mars's atmosphere, among the most important being solar wind.

The Sun is constantly emitting photons (sub-atomic particles which travel incredibly fast), electrons and radioactive alpha particles, that all make up the solar wind.

The photons smash into atoms in Mars's atmosphere, forming charged particles. With the loss of most of Mars's magnetic field, these charged particles have been carried off into space (a process called 'sputtering'). Billions of years ago, when the Sun was much younger, sputtering would have been happening at a much faster rate, and this is what's thought to have swept away over 65% of Mars's original atmosphere.

What little atmosphere remains means there is far less protection on the surface of Mars from the solar wind's radiation. Sudden pulses of radiation are emitted by the Sun when it produces solar flares and mass ejections. These can be extremely dangerous to all forms of life (including humans), as they can strip atoms apart, alter DNA, produce potentially fatal radiation sickness and cause cancers.

Although Earth loses hundred of tonnes of atmosphere every day due to radiation and sputtering, it has its own magnetic field which pushes most solar wind around the planet and as a result, our atmosphere does not get pummeled by the solar wind so much.

Mars's Present Day Atmospherics and Features

Sunrises and sunsets occur at the start and end of each Martian day, but the Sun appears much smaller as Mars is that much further away. This is why it's much colder too. Owing to the atmosphere being so thin, the oranges and reds familiar to us at these times of day are missing, and what might be called 'the sky' has no blue colour to it at all.

Clouds on Mars are generally rare. The thin atmosphere and the scarcity of water mean that the conditions for clouds to form do not occur very often. The best time for clouds is during the coldest months and near the Martian equator. They tend to appear about 60 km up and are formed from water ice. Any that are higher may be made of dry ice (frozen CO_2). Vortexes also occur around the poles.

Auroras have also been recorded on Mars due to the virtually nonexistent magnetic field. Martian Auroras produce ultraviolet light, so can only be detected by scientific instruments and not by the human eye.

Whilst the weather on Mars is quite different to that on Earth, some strong and often relentless winds do occur. In 2001, Mars experienced a global dust storm that raged for months, with the atmosphere of much of the planet remaining hazy for weeks afterwards. Typical wind speeds are between 16-32 km/hr but speeds of 113 km/hr have also been recorded.

On occasion, localised winds are so strong that they whip up the surface dust into tornadoes which have been nicknamed 'dust devils'. They form when the CO_2-rich air close to the surface is heated by sunlight, which rises and then interacts with the cooler air higher up. The largest ones can reach a height of 8 km (much higher than tornadoes can reach on Earth), but they only last a short time, from 1-20 minutes in duration.

Their presence on Mars was discovered by chance in 2004. Two rovers, *Spirit* and *Opportunity*, landed on opposite sides of the planet in January of that year. It was believed that their solar panels would gradually become covered with Martian dust, resulting in their mission times being limited to just three months. It was hoped, however, that periodic Martian winds would help to blow some of the dust off the panels from time to time and extend their mission times. This did indeed happen, but on 12th March 2005, *Spirit's* power suddenly and unexpectedly surged from ~60% to 93%. The rover's cameras managed to

A Martian sunset taken by the *Curiosity* rover on April 15th, 2015.
Consider the immensity of the technological achievement
of photographing a sunset on another planet.

record, for the first time, a fortuitous close encounter with a dust devil, whose strong winds completely cleaned the panels of dust.

Amazingly, *Spirit* continued exploring until 2011 (when it got stuck in soft sand); and *Opportunity* kept going until mid-2018!

Martian 'spiders' (or araneiforms) is a description given to a type of terrain characterised by multiple channels radiating out from a point, thus resembling the legs of a spider.

They're found near the South Pole on Mars where temperatures are cold enough for CO_2 to solidify (-78 °C) and form 'dry-ice' sheets.

In springtime, the Sun gradually heats up the ground beneath these ice sheets, causing the dry-ice to sublimate (turning straight from a solid to a gas without a liquid phase).

Pressure then builds up underneath the dry-ice which leads to the ice sheet cracking around a central eruption of CO_2. In some places, these erupting plumes bring with them darkened dust from the ground beneath.

In 2016, NASA conducted a 'citizen science' project, asking people to look for 'spiders' from South Pole images taken by the *Mars Reconnaissance Orbiter*.

Over 10,000 contributors managed to identify 20 new areas for further investigation.

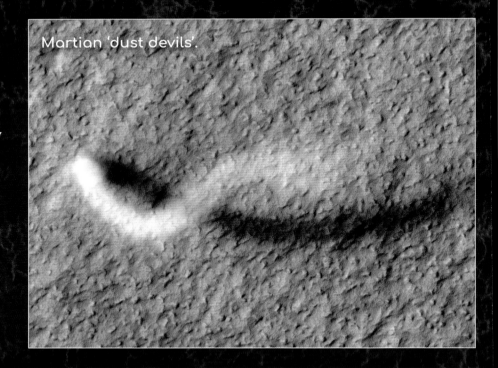

Martian 'dust devils'.

Sand dunes in polar regions of Mars show light coatings of pale orange dust blown partially across the dark basaltic sand. Around the edges of the dunes, patches of seasonal dry ice remain.

Mars' enigmatic eruption plumes.

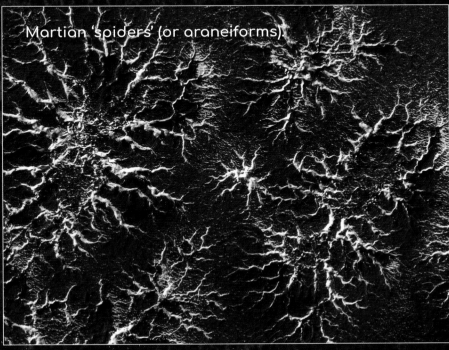

Martian 'spiders' (or araneiforms)

Colonising Mars

NASA has set the ambitious goal of sending astronauts to land on Mars by the end of the 2030s.

If this goal is achieved, it will represent a landmark in human history. Imagine humans walking across another world. Think of the discoveries that could be made - the advancements in science and the implications for industry, society and culture.

But the logistics and complexities of travelling to Mars are immense. The journey to Mars will take six to nine months (depending upon how far apart Earth and Mars are in their orbits, at the time of travel).

The entire mission is likely to span several years.

Could you cope with that? With not being able to make physical contact with loved ones for that long, even though there would probably be video-calls to Earth regularly? However, these might have to be in the form of one-way 'news packages', as immediate two-way conversations would be thwarted by transmission delays.

The selection of suitable astronauts will be equally as important as developing advanced technologies.

Despite the challenges, if successful, this mission could be the most important journey of discovery in human history.

Radiation

In spite of our rapidly increasing knowledge about the red planet, Mars remains a very hostile place for humans. Ensuring adequate protection from radiation will be paramount.

There are two main types of radiation: non-ionising and ionising. Non-ionising radiation has enough energy to move atoms in a molecule around or cause them to vibrate, but not enough to remove electrons from atoms. Examples of this kind of radiation are radio waves, visible light and microwaves.

Ionising radiation has so much energy it can knock electrons out of atoms. It can affect the atoms in living things, so it poses a health risk by damaging tissue and the DNA in genes. Ionizing radiation comes from x-ray machines, cosmic particles from outer space and radioactive elements.

The Sun, however, is not wholly responsible for all the radiation in our Solar System. Some particles, known as galactic cosmic rays, travel through space even faster than those emitted from the Sun. These particles may have been produced millions of years ago, possibly from a supernova. They will pass through a spaceship or a human body unimpeded, and atoms they collide with are likely to be ionised.

On Earth, we are shielded to a large extent by our planet's magnetic field. This deflects the vast majority of these cosmic rays. We are also protected by our atmosphere, whose particles interfere with the cosmic rays and mostly nullify them.

It will be important to protect astronauts during their journey to Mars from these cosmic rays. Scientists are currently looking at the best way to do this. Luckily, the spacecraft's structure will provide a shield from those coming from the Sun. However, high energy waves and galactic cosmic radiation will pass straight through the walls of the spacecraft. The best element to stop this radiation is hydrogen, and one idea is to store water (H_2O) in the walls of the craft (though this would add weight too).

To minimise the exposure of humans to harmful radiation of all forms, as much preparatory work as possible would need to be done by autonomous vehicles and robots before a human could set foot on Mars. This means there would need to be quite a few missions featuring more rovers and other robotic machines being sent to the planet before the end of the 2030s (if the existing timetable is to be kept to).

Human Settlements on Mars

Reasons for colonising Mars include curiosity and scientific discovery (the potential for humans to provide more in-depth observational research than unmanned rovers; economic interest in its resources) and the possibility that the settlement of other planets could decrease the likelihood of human extinction.

For humans to survive any length of time in any hostile environment (be it on Earth, in space or on another planet), we must have access to four basic requirements: water, oxygen, food and shelter.

Might humans land on Mars in the near future?

HOW WOULD WE GET WATER?

Water is essential for all forms of life, whether it's for microbes or human astronauts. We know there is water on Mars but almost all of it is in the form of ice, with small amounts being held by hydrated chemicals in the soil, and even smaller amounts existing within the atmosphere. The north polar ice cap has vast amounts of water-ice on the surface but would it be accessible? It's also present beneath the permanent CO_2 ice cap at the south pole. Be that as it may, obtaining small amounts of water from the Martian soil seems to be the most likely source that will be used, although drilling boreholes through the surface layers to underground lakes (if any can be located) is also a possibility.

It is probable that any colony would be located where the water content of the soil is at its highest, most probably between latitudes 40°- 45° North. (Because of the lower height of the terrain here, it is also where atmospheric pressure is at its greatest). Water extractor units would heat the soil until the water evaporates. The evaporated water would then be condensed and stored. Ideally, a minimum of 5 l/person/day would be required. Recycling as much of this water as possible would also be very important.

HOW WOULD WE GET OXYGEN?

A reliable supply of oxygen could be obtained from the electrolysis of water (H_2O). The oxygen gas produced would need to be mixed with nitrogen gas (and other trace gases) to produce a breathable gas that was not toxic for humans. The hydrogen produced as a 'by-product' of the electrolysis process could be refined into 'hydrozene' for use as a fuel.

Another way of obtaining oxygen would be from the CO_2 in the Martian atmosphere, of which there's plenty! The *Perseverance* rover currently on Mars has a dedicated experiment on board to see whether this process would work and how much energy it would require. Another source might be perchlorate, present in Martian soil, which is also rich in oxygen (see below).

HOW WOULD WE GET FOOD?

Sustaining a small colony on Mars would require food being produced by the colony in some way. It would be expensive and inefficient to expect regular supplies of food to come from Earth. Which begs the question - could plants be farmed on Mars? Whilst there would be numerous difficulties to overcome, most Mars experts believe this would be possible.

Hydroponic cultivation of crops.

Let us assume that water would not be a limiting factor in growing crops. Certainly a constant supply of water (which could be recycled) would be a must. We'd also need to know if Martian soil was suitable for growing crops. Would all plants be grown using hydroponics (in other words, soil-free), or would soil of some sort be required?

Whilst the finer particles of regolith would provide a suitable medium for the roots of plants to gain traction, the minerals it contains are not all beneficial ones. It is already known that such soil is high in calcium perchlorate (a molecule formed from calcium, chlorine and oxygen atoms), making it toxic. Scientists have already proposed a biochemical extraction technique to separate out the perchlorate which would be energetically cheap, environmentally friendly and could be used to obtain oxygen both for human consumption and to fuel surface operations.

Experiments undertaken recently by scientists at Wageningen University in the Netherlands showed that crops grew well in artificial soil but only if there was fertilser and organic matter included in the mix. They used grass cuttings (composted by bacteria), but on Mars it would more likely come from treated human waste.

It's likely that a mix of both hydroponics and treated regolith would probably be used as growing media. As natural sunlight on Mars is only about 50% as strong as it is on Earth (further away, yet with a clear atmosphere), artificial lighting would be used as part of fully automated controlled growing conditions.

Between 2014 and 2016, astronauts experimented with growing salad crops such as red lettuce on board the *International Space Station*. As these astronauts had to cope with freeze-dried ice cream, liquid salt and pepper and dehydrated prawn cocktail, fresh vegetables were found to make a pleasant change!

Space food is constantly improving, but even so, astronauts can get fed up of eating the same vacuum-packed meals. Typically, astronauts return from the *ISS* having lost weight, not necessarily from eating less but associated with zero-gravity reduced muscle and bone mass.

WHAT WOULD SHELTERS BE LIKE ON MARS?

As radiation on Mars is a big problem, shielding from it will be really important. Even cancer-inducing ultraviolet sunlight will penetrate through the thin atmosphere. Any type of shelter (or 'habitat') built on the Martian surface would need to be designed to minimise penetrating radiation to protect crew.

Internal spaces would need to be pressurised and filled with breathable air. Any excursions from these 'pods' would require air-locks, spaces where spacesuits can be donned on or off, as well as the fitting of helmets and breathing tanks.

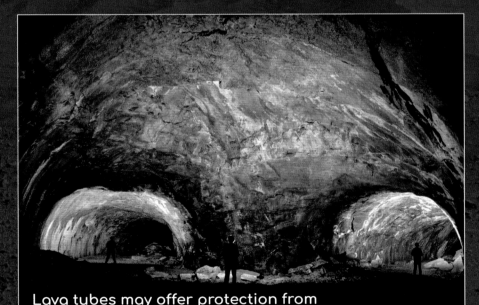

Lava tubes may offer protection from radiation for future settlements on Mars. Shown here is the Lava River Cave, Arizona.

Buildings would have to be strong enough to withstand dust storms, warm enough to combat the low (often sub-zero temperatures), and thick enough to negate as much radiation as possible.

Lava tubes, volcanic caverns that are formed by fast-moving lava flows associated with shield volcanoes, are known to be present beneath the surface at some regions on Mars. They occur on Earth, but those on Mars are bigger due to gravity only being a third of what it is on Earth. Such tunnels could provide ideal locations for habitats to be built within them, as the rock above would provide ready-made radiation protection, shelter from dust storms as well as insulation. Perhaps these would provide living quarters while surface habitats associated with workshops, storage, or launch sites were being built.

Who would be building these habitats? It's likely to be autonomous machines with the ability to undertake 3-D printing on a grand scale. Modified regolith would be used as the main building material, perhaps mixed with some added adhesive. Several such mobile machines would work on the same building, gradually adding layer upon layer to a pre-specified shape.

In 2015, a Dutch company (Mars One) proposed sending four volunteer astronauts to Mars on a one-way mission, for a landing in 2024 (later put back to 2032). Interestingly, 2,700 people applied for the posts but the mission will never happen as the company went bust in 2019. Would you be willing to volunteer for such a trip?

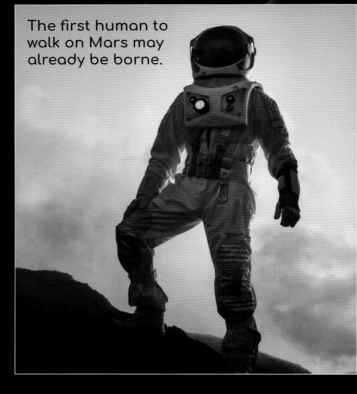

The first human to walk on Mars may already be borne.

Can we Terraform Mars?

Science fiction writers have long dreamt of using technology to transform Mars into a second Earth. One where humans could live without the need for spacesuits, and crops could be grown across the Martian landscape. NASA has undertaken serious studies to explore this possibility.

Imagine the implications of humankind becoming an interplanetary species. With a second habitable world, we would have a safeguard against global calamity on Earth, and many of the problems might be alleviated, such as overpopulation and dwindling resources.

Terraforming Mars would entail three major interconnected changes: increasing the density and composition of the atmosphere, raising the global temperature and building up the magnetosphere.

Mars's atmosphere is currently unbreathable, being just 1% of the density of Earth's atmosphere and consisting mostly of carbon dioxide (with small amounts of nitrogen, argon and various trace gases).

Significant quantities of carbon dioxide and other insulative gases are locked up in the Martian polar caps and regolith. If these reserves could be released, the atmosphere would thicken, creating a greenhouse effect, trapping in heat and warming the planet.

The melting of Mars' polar ice caps would also release vast quantities of water which would eventually form oceans across the planet (see p. 83), which would further absorb energy from sunlight and raise the global temperature.

Oceanic water and a warmer atmosphere would lead to the formation of clouds, rainfall, moisture and more fertile regolith, more conducive conditions for plant life, which may eventually yield a higher proportion of oxygen in the atmosphere. An artificial magnetosphere could then be generated using electric currents to protect the atmosphere.

Although the above steps are theoretically possible using current technology, most of the studies undertaken suggest the atmosphere of Mars could only be thickened to about 7% of Earth's, and thousands of years would be needed for Mars to support even the most hardy 'extremophile' forms of life on Earth. For now, Mars will remain a cold, dry, frozen world, but perhaps future technologies may truly make terraforming the red planet a possibility.

Could terraforming Mars create a second world for humans to inhabit?

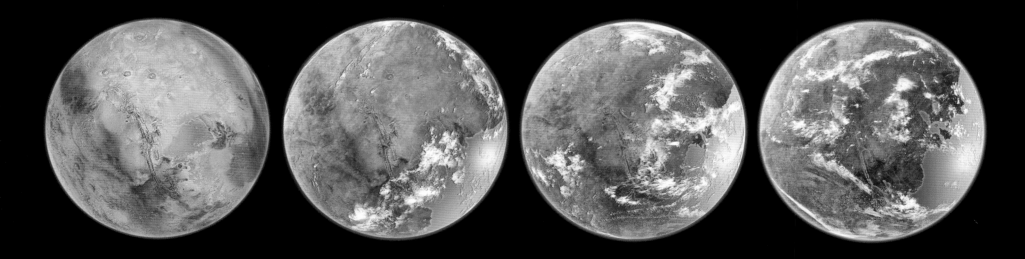

A NASA rocket blasts off.

A cargo spacecraft in low-Earth orbit.

A SpaceX Starship.

THE NEXT CHAPTER

The dream of establishing a base on the Moon and sending astronauts throughout the Solar System faded after the *Apollo* programme came to an end in 1972.

But the last decade has seen greater innovation in space technology than the previous five decades combined. Much of the progress has been driven by private companies developing reusable rockets.

Almost all major rockets built before the 21st century were designed to undertake a single flight (often consisting of multiple stages that detach and burn up on re-entry into the Earth's atmosphere). Single use rockets are comparable to throwing away a brand new jumbo jet after a single journey.

The advent of reusable components, which includes booster rockets that detach and safely land on launch pads, as well as main launch vehicles which reliably return to land on Earth, opens the possibility of space journeys at a fraction of former costs, because these vehicles are essentially able to fly again after being refueled. Instead of building a new rocket for every single flight, the main cost is simply fuel.

The design of reusable rockets has been driven by Elon Musk, and his pioneering company SpaceX, with which NASA is working in preparation for the upcoming *Artemis* Programme.

The primary goal of the *Artemis* Programme is to return humans to the Moon by 2025, specifically to explore the lunar south pole. It includes the establishment of a permanent research base on the Moon, at which astronauts can develop technologies and lay the foundation for the extraction of resources in the hope of eventually making crewed missions to Mars and beyond possible.

The *Artemis* Programme is led by NASA, but undertaken in partnership with the European Space Agency, the UK Space Agency, the Japanese Space Agency and partnerships with many other nations. This dawning of a new era of space exploration is the most exciting chapter in the history of space science.

Follow the next steps in space science via online videos on the Astrum YouTube channel. Scan the following QR code or search 'Astrum' on **www.youtube.com**

IMAGE CREDITS

ASU = Arizona State University.

CIT = California Institute of Technology.

CIW = Carnegie Institution of Washington.

ESA = European Space Agency.

ESO = European Southern Observatory.

ESO's VLT = European Southern Observatory's Very Large Telescope.

JAXA = Japan Aerospace Exploration Agency.

JPL = Jet Propulsion Laboratory.

JHUAPL = Johns Hopkins University Applied Physics Laboratory.

MSSS = Malin Space Science Systems.

NASA = National Aeronautics and Space Administration.

SDO = Solar Dynamics Observatory.

SS = Shutterstock.

STScI = Space Telescope Science Institute.

Front Cover: NASA/Seán Doran https://www.flickr.com/photos/seandoran. Front Endpaper: NASA/Seán Doran https://www.flickr.com/photos/seandoran. 1: NASA/Seán Doran https://www.flickr.com/photos/seandoran. 2: ESO's VLT/ESO/Digitized Sky Survey 2. 3: Nebula - NASA images/SS. 4: HebenPhilis/SS. 5: HebenPhilis/SS. 6: Denis Belitsky/SS. 7: ESO's VLT/ESO/Digitized Sky Survey 2. 8: Background - ESO's VLT/ESO/Digitized Sky Survey 2, Diagram of the observable Universe by Pablo Budassi graphic design and musical productions. 9: Background - ESO's VLT/ESO/Digitized Sky Survey 2, Diagram of the observable Universe by Pablo Budassi graphic design and musical productions. 10: Background - ESO's VLT/ESO/Digitized Sky Survey 2. 11, 12, 13, 14, 15, 16, 17, 18, 19: On all of these pages - Diagram of Observable Universe by Andrew Z. Colvin/wikipedia - CC BY-SA 4.0 - https://creativecommons.org/licenses/by-sa/4.0/ - minor changes made for including in this book, Background - ESO's VLT/ESO/Digitized Sky Survey 2. 20: Background - ESO's VLT/ESO/Digitized Sky Survey 2. 21: NASA, ESA, J. Hester and A. Loll (Arizona State University) - HubbleSite. 22: Background - ESO's VLT/ESO/Digitized Sky Survey 2. 23: Background - ESO's VLT/ESO/Digitized Sky Survey 2, Dotted Yeti/SS. 24: Background - ESO's VLT/ESO/Digitized Sky Survey 2. 25: Background - ESO's VLT/ESO/Digitized Sky Survey 2, Kateryna Kon/SS. 26: Background - ESO's VLT/ESO/Digitized Sky Survey 2. 27: Background - ESO's VLT/ESO/Digitized Sky Survey 2, shooarts/SS (with elements from NASA, JPL, ESA and JAXA). 28: Background - ESO's VLT/ESO/Digitized Sky Survey 2, ibreakstock/SS (with elements from NASA, JPL, ESA and JAXA). 29: NASA by Bricktop; edited by Deuar, KFP, TotoBaggins, City303, JCPag2015 - solarsystem.nasa.gov. 30-31: Background - ESO's VLT/ESO/Digitized Sky Survey 2 (with elements from NASA, JPL, ESA and JAXA). 32: Saturn V rockets courtesy of NASA Apollo program, V2 rockets (left) Bundesarchiv, Bild 141-1880 / CC-BY-SA 3.0 and (right) Bundesarchiv, RH8II Bild-B0788-42 BSM / CC-BY-SA 3.0. 33: Background - ESO's VLT/ESO/Digitized Sky Survey 2. 34: Background - ESO's VLT/ESO/Digitized Sky Survey 2. 35: Both images - NASA Apollo program. 36-37: all images - NASA Apollo program. 38: NASA/Everett Collection/SS. 39: Background - ESO's VLT/ESO/Digitized Sky Survey 2. 40: Background - ESO's VLT/ESO/Digitized Sky Survey 2. 41: Background - ESO's VLT/ESO/Digitized Sky Survey 2, Hubble telescope courtesy of NASA/STScI/ESA, International Space Station - NASA/Boeing/STScI/ESA. 42: Background - ESO's VLT/ESO/Digitized Sky Survey 2, Rovers by NASA, JPL, CIT. 43: AleksandrMorrisovich/SS. 44-45: NASA/SDO. 46: NASA/SDO. 47: Background and cut out of sun - NASA/SDO, diagram Kelvinsong/wikipedia - CC BY-SA 3.0. 48-49: NASA/SDO. 50-51: NASA/JHUAPL/ASU/CIW. 52: NASA/JHUAPL/ASU/CIW. 53: NASA/JHUAPL/ASU/CIW, Earth - NASA - Apollo Program. 54: Background - NASA/JHUAPL/ASU/CIW, Transit of Mercury by Elijah Mathews/wikipedia - CC BY-SA 4.0, surface of Mercury - NASA/JHUAPL/ASU/CIW. 55: Background - NASA/JHUAPL/ASU/CIW. 56: Background - NASA/JHUAPL/ASU/CIW, Picasso Crater - NASA/JHUAPL/CIW, North Pole of Mercury - NASA. 57: Background - NASA/JHUAPL/ASU/CIW, Mercury - NASA. 58-59: NASA. 60: JAXA probe Akatsuki. 61: Background - NASA, images of Mercury and Earth - NASA/JHUAPL/ASU/CIW, Earth - NASA - Apollo Program. 62: Background and two images of Mercury NASA/JHUAPL/ASU/CIW, Mariner program and Magellan program. 63: Background - NASA. 64: Background - JAXA probe Akatsuki, model of Venera 1 by Armael/wikipedia - CC0 1.0, Venera 9 by Government of the USSR / Venera 9 mission, Venera 13 by Government of the USSR / Venera 13 mission. 65: Background - JAXA probe Akatsuki. 66-67: NASA/Seán Doran https://www.flickr.com/photos/seandoran. 68: Earth - NASA - Apollo Program. 69: Background - 168 STUDIO/SS, images of Earth - NASA - Apollo Program. 70: Background - NASA/Seán Doran https://www.flickr.com/photos/seandoran. 71: Background - NASA/Seán Doran https://www.flickr.com/photos/seandoran, diagram of Earth's structure: Vadim Sadovski/SS. 72: NASA. 73: NASA. 74: Background - elRoce/SS, acarapi/SS, 1249664152/SS, wichitpong katwit/SS. 75: Background - elRoce/SS, Kurit Afshen/SS, Gualberto Becerra, Damsea/SS. 76: NASA Viking program. 77: NASA Viking program. 78: Mars - ESA & MPS for OSIRIS Team MPS/UPD/LAM/IAA/RSSD/INTA/UPM/DASP/IDA. 79: Background - NASA, images of Mars - ESA & MPS for OSIRIS Team MPS/UPD/LAM/IAA/RSSD/INTA/UPM/DASP/IDA, Image of Earth - NASA Apollo program. 80: NASA/JPL - Curiosity program. 81: Background NASA/JPL - Curiosity program, diagram of Mars's geological structure AlexLMX/SS. 82: NASA HiRISE. 83: Background - NASA HiRISE, ESA Mars Express program. 84: NASA HiRISE, ESA Mars Express program. 85: NASA HiRISE, ESA Mars Express program. 86: ESA's Rosetta mission. 87: Background - NASA/JPL-Caltech/UCLA/MPS/DLR/IDA, diagram of near Earth Object NASA/JPS/Caltech, Asteroid 243 Ida - NASA Galileo prob/JPL/Processed by Kevin M. Gill/wikipedia/ CC BY-SA 2.0. 88-89: NASA/Seán Doran https://www.flickr.com/photos/seandoran. 90: Jupiter - Hubble telescope courtesy of NASA/STScI/ESA. 91: Background - NASA Cassini probe. Images of Jupiter - Hubble telescope courtesy of NASA/STScI/ESA. 92: Background - NASA/Seán Doran https://www.flickr.com/photos/seandoran. 93: Background and insert - NASA/Seán Doran https://www.flickr.com/photos/seandoran. 94: Background - joshimerbin/SS, Image of Red Spot - NASA/ESA, Size comparison with earth NASA/Seán Doran https://www.flickr.com/photos/seandoran. 95: Top left - NASA, ESA, and A. Simon (Goddard Space Flight Center) , top right - NASA, ESA, and J. Nichols (University of Leicester), bottom left NASA Hubble Space Telescope/International Gemini Observatory/NOIRLab/NSF/AURA, M.H. Wong (UC Berkeley)/wikipedia CC BY 4.0., bottom right NASA Hubble Space Telescope/International Gemini Observatory/NOIRLab/NSF/AURA, M.H. Wong (UC Berkeley)/wikipedia CC BY 4.0. 96: Background - NASA/Seán Doran https://www.flickr.com/photos/seandoran, moons - NASA/JPL/DLR - http://photojournal.jpl.nasa.gov/catalog/PIA01299. 97: Background - NASA/Seán Doran https://www.flickr.com/photos/seandoran, bottom left NASA/JPL, bottom right NASA/JPL-Caltech/SETI Institute. 98: Background - NASA / JPLab-Caltech/SETI Institute. Two illustrations - NASA/JPL-Caltech, black smoker vents - U.S. National Oceanic and Atmospheric Administration. 99: NASA / JPLab-Caltech / SETI Institute. 100: Background - NASA/Seán Doran https://www.flickr.com/photos/seandoran, insert NASA/JPL/University of Arizona. 101: Background - NASA/Seán Doran https://www.flickr.com/photos/seandoran. 102, 103, 104, 105, 106, 107, 108, 109: All images - Cassini orbiter - NASA/JPL-Caltech/SSI. 110: Background - Cassini orbiter, NASA/JPL-Caltech/SSI. 111: Background - Cassini orbiter, NASA/JPL-Caltech/SSI, Titan - Cassini orbiter, NASA/JPL-Caltech/SSI, - surface of titan, surface of Titan by Huygens probe - ESA, NASA, JPL, University of Arizona, illustration of Enceladus - NASA, JPL-Caltech, Space Science Institute. 112, 113, 114, 115: All images of Uranus by Voyager 2 probe - NASA/JPL. 116: Background - Voyager 2 probe - NASA/JPL. 117: Background - Voyager 2 probe - NASA/JPL, two inserts of Uranus by Hubble Space Telescope's NICMOS camera - NASA Marshall Space Flight Center. 118: Background - StudioFI/SS, insert Voyager 2 probe - NASA/JPL. 119: Background - StudioFI/SS, insert Voyager 2 probe - NASA/JPL,Miranda by Voyager 2 probe - NASA/JPL. 120, 121, 122, 123, 124, 125, 126, 127: All images of Neptune by Voyager 2 probe - NASA/JPL/Voyager-ISS/Caltech/Justin Cowart. 128, 129, 130, 131, 132, 133, 134, 135: All images by New Horizons probe - NASA/Johns Hopkins University Applied Physics Laboratory/Southwest Research Institute/Alex Parker. 136, 137: NASA/JPL - Curiosity program. 138, 139: NASA/JPL - Curiosity program. 140: Background - NASA HiRISE. 141: Background - NASA HiRISE. left fukume/SS, top right - ESA Mars Express program, bottom right - elRoce/SS. 142: Background - NASA HiRISE. 143: Background - NASA HiRISE. topographic diagram - Mars Orbiter Laser Altimeter (MOLA) Team, MGS Project, NASA. 144: Background - NASA HiRISE, inserts NASA/ JPL - Curiosity program. 145: NASA HiRISE. 146: NASA HiRISE. 147: NASA/JPL - Curiosity program. 148, 149: All images - NASA HiRISE. 150: Background - NASA HiRISE. 151: Background - NASA HiRISE. 3Dsculptor/SS. 152: Background - NASA HiRISE, Nikolay_E/SS. 153: Background - NASA HiRISE, Michael Landrum/SS. 154: Background - NASA HiRISE, Gorodenkoff/SS. 155: Background - NASA HiRISE, Stockbym/SS. 156: Top left - Oleg_Yakovlev/SS, bottom left - Paopano/SS, right - Jared Krahn/wikipedia - CC BY-SA 4.0. 157, 158, 159 and 160: Background - ESO's VLT/ESO/Digitized Sky Survey 2. Inserts on 159 by Alex McColgan, Brad Wilson and Robert Irving. Back Endpaper: NASA/Seán Doran https://www.flickr.com/photos/seandoran. Back Cover: Nebula - NASA images/SS; Mars - ESA & MPS for OSIRIS Team MPS/UPD/LAM/IAA/RSSD/INTA/UPM/DASP/IDA, Rover - NASA; Curiosity Rover, MSSS/JPL.CIT; Sun - NASA/GSFC/SDO; Background Image - Denis Belitsky/SS.

ABOUT THE AUTHORS

Alex McColgan

Alex started the Astrum YouTube channel in 2013 as a mix of his passions: film making and space science. Astrum has now become one of the leading channels on space on the platform, with over 115 million views and nearly 1 million subscribers. Alex's content covers a wide range of space and astronomy subjects, from the geography of planets in our Solar System, to human exploration and the latest discoveries by the leading space agencies. Much of the content of the Astrum channel has also been translated into other languages, including Chinese, Spanish and Portuguese. Born in Wales, Alex is married and has a beautiful daughter.

Stewart McPherson

Stewart is a naturalist, author and film-maker. He spent a decade climbing 300 mountains across the world to study carnivorous plants to write a series of 30 books. Along the way, he co-discovered and co-named 35 new taxa. He travelled to all of the UK Overseas Territories to film the TV series *Britain's Treasure Islands*, and then sailed around the UK in a tall ship to explore the most remote British Isles to film the series *Britain's Secret Island*. Working with the Don Hanson Charitable Foundation and the Jane Goodall Institute Australia, he has created and sent resource boxes to more than 50,000 schools in the UK and Australia to drive passion for nature and conservation. See www.stewartmcpherson.tv

Robert Irving

Robert has spent most of his working life as a marine biologist, though he spent his early career as a primary school teacher and has always had a fascination with the night sky and our place in the Universe. He has worked with Stewart McPherson on a number of projects, particularly as an editor and as a contributing author. He has always had a broad interest in the natural world and, besides several scientific papers, has written books on the marine life of Sussex; on the history of the UK's first Marine Protected Area around the island of Lundy; and is currently working on a field guide to the wildlife of the Pitcairn Islands in the South Pacific.

INDEX